BARRIO WALK: STEPPING INTO WISDOM

Mike and Paulette:

Wishing you the best always.

God bless you.

Ruben

SDG

BARRIO WALK: STEPPING INTO WISDOM

Ruben Gonzales

ELM HILL

A Division of
HarperCollins Christian Publishing

www.elmhillbooks.com

Barrio Walk: Stepping Into Wisdom

Published in Nashville, Tennessee, by Elm Hill, an imprint of Thomas Nelson. Elm Hill and Thomas Nelson are registered trademarks of HarperCollins Christian Publishing, Inc.

Elm Hill titles may be purchased in bulk for educational, business, fund-raising, or sales promotional use. For information, please e-mail SpecialMarkets@ ThomasNelson.com.

All Scripture quotations, unless otherwise indicated, are taken from the Holy Bible, New International Version®, NIV®. Copyright © 1973, 1978, 1984, 2011 by Biblica, Inc.° Used by permission of Zondervan. All rights reserved worldwide. www.Zondervan. com. The "NIV" and "New International Version" are trademarks registered in the United States Patent and Trademark Office by Biblica, Inc.°

Library of Congress Cataloging-in-Publication Data

Library of Congress Control Number: 2019912392

ISBN 978-1-400327737 (HardBound)
ISBN 978-1-400327720 (Paperback)
ISBN 978-1-400327744 (eBook)

Contents

CHAPTER 1

MOCKING THE ROOSTER

Things in the barrio happen quickly. The slower you learn to adapt; the rougher life becomes. For every decision you make there are always consequences, especially if it involves disobedience. Walk with me through my barrio so I can share some lessons learned along the way.

The year was 1957 and even though we lived in the center of Phoenix, our next-door neighbors raised chickens in their backyard. My mother always warned me to stay away from our neighbors' yard birds. Mom was always busy cooking for a family of six and doing her best at managing the household finances. She was extremely strict, and when she finished lecturing me, she would say, "Let's see what kind of travesura (mischief) you get into today."

My mother was raised by her grandmother who was half Native American from the Chemehuevi tribe. This tribe is part of a reservation near Parker, Arizona. My mother told me her grandmother was extremely strict and abusive. She also said my great grandmother liked me more than my brothers because I was more fair-skinned than them. Hmm? Perhaps she had what Native Americans refer to as the apple syndrome—red on the outside and white on the inside. I faintly remember her giving me whole tomatoes from a can after she sprinkled sugar on them. The day my "magrande" (big mom), as mom would call her, died was a sad day for everyone. She fell when watering her yard and her head struck something hard.

My mother told me (I was too young to remember) magrande would sing to me as an infant. She would sing, "Baila, baila, como un penguino baila, baila" which means "dance, dance, like a penguin dances, dance." My mother said I would wobble dance for my magrande before I learned how to walk. So, since those early days of shaking my tailfeathers, one of my lifelong nicknames is penguino.

At that point in my young life, I was not quite five years old and spent a lot of my time entertaining my younger three-year-old sister named Lupe. She was lanky and not comfortable walking on uneven surfaces. Her manner of walking outdoors looked like a newborn colt taking its first steps, sort of like Bambi on ice. We did not get to spend much time outside without adult presence. We were both at an age where our curiosity seemed to keep us locked up in trouble. One of my favorite things to do was to show off for "Lupeanuts," the nickname I gave her.

On this particular day, I decided to demonstrate to her how the rooster walks. As we slowly walked down our neighbors' dilapidated sidewalk, we were careful not to step on any of the plants they were growing. There was a damp and musky smell because our neighbors grew whatever they could wherever there was dirt. They had *hierba buena* (mint), cilantro, jalapenos, and tomatoes. I told Lupe to stay back as I stretched my legs and struggled to straddle over the small fence quickly so I would not be seen by my mother.

When I saw the rooster strutting, I went into a conceited stroll of my own. My head bobbed while I stretched my imaginary wings and raked the ground with my feet. My sister laughed as she enjoyed my rooster imitation act. I felt like I was about to sprout feathers and could hardly wait for the next sunrise.

Much later in life I learned, "There are three things that are stately in their stride, ... a lion, mighty among beasts, who retreats before nothing; a *strutting rooster*, and a he-goat" (Proverbs 30:30–31).

All of a sudden, I looked up and was staring eye to eye with a rooster that did not like being mocked. He had a look in his eyes that said, "oh heck no!" I made a futile attempt to intimidate the cock by giving him my fiercest mean mug look. It did not work as the stupid rooster went into attack mode. It scared me into running faster than my little legs could go and I fell to the ground. To this day, I'm not sure if I fell on my own or the rooster gave me a flying double kick. That no-good yard bird proceeded to do a tap dance on my back and pecked me like a large corn on the cob. I screamed while the rooster bit and scratched me for an eternity (probably less than half a minute).

Our neighbor, Chavela, heard the commotion and ran out of her house with her broom swinging. She yelled, "Gallo condenado, te voy a matar!" That means, "You sorry rooster, I am going to kill you!" Chavela was animated and always wore a bandana like Rosie the Riveter. She spoke in a rapid-fire vocabulary that mixed choppy English with Spanish. She picked me up and rushed me into our house. Chavela apologized profusely, and I remember my mother saying, "It's his own fault, I told him to stay away from the rooster."

They laid me on the bed and brought out the sangre de chango (monkey's blood), also known as iodine, to put on my injuries. This hurt more than the rooster's pecks and scratches. As they applied the iodine on my back with the stiff plastic applicator, I squirmed liked a worm being impaled on a fishhook. Chavela tried to distract me with one of her favorite sayings. She said, "My husband esta tan viejo (is so old), he doesn't let me buy him green bananas." She was laughing before she could finish the sentence, and I had no clue what she was talking about.

Later that evening, Chavela and her husband Eleazar invited all of us to their house for dinner. Chavela had prepared for us some arroz con pollo (chicken with rice); in this case, it was arroz con gallo (rooster with rice). The meal was by far the best dead chicken I had ever tasted. We did not use napkins back in those days, and everyone passed around the same cloth napkin which was usually a dish drying towel. Prior to the meal, my mother told me and my two older brothers she did not want to hear a word out of us except for, "thank you, Mr. and Mrs. Ramirez." We were on our best behavior. My oldest brother and I had been known to just look at each other and start laughing. Our most recent occasion was during a rosary held at our house.

During the meal, Chavela enjoyed telling everyone the story of how she looked outside and saw the rooster scratching and pecking me on the ground. She was talking fast and would barely stop to take a breath. Her story was colorful, and she even threw in a few choice, extra cuss words other than "gallo condenado." She went on to describe how much she enjoyed twisting the rooster's head off and pulling off his feathers con ganas (with gusto) while getting it ready for our meal.

When we finished eating, Chavela hugged me and told me I would not have to worry about the rooster anymore. She took me outside to show me the rooster's decapitated head that she had discarded in her backyard. I was afraid to get too close to the rooster's head because his eyes were bugged out and had a look of confusion. From a safe distance, I pointed at the rooster and stuck my tongue out; I laughed and yelled out, "Ha! Ha!" I hugged Chavela and told her, "Thank you for saving me and the food was good too."

Later that night, before going to bed, I imitated the rooster one last time for my sister Lupe. She laughed as she saw me attempt to strut with a hunched, hurt back. At the end of the day, even though the rooster won the battle, I won the war (thanks to Chavela). This makes me more than a conqueror because I went to bed with a smile while burping rooster.

It was difficult to sleep that night because it was hot and my back was irritated. My mind kept reliving the terror of being helpless against the rooster. I cried silently and wished I had obeyed my mother and stayed away from the rooster. Hmmm... maybe that's why the good book says, "Children *obey* your parents in the Lord, for this pleases the Lord" (Ephesians 6:1).

Even today, more than sixty years later, Lupe will occasionally tease me by saying, "Hey Ruuster," instead of Ruben.

Barrio lesson # 1 Never mess with a rooster you can't outrun.

CHAPTER 2

GAINING UNDERSTANDING

My mother told me when she was trying to wean me from the bottle, she tried some unconventional methods that I'm sure are not recommended by the *Reader's Digest*. She would hide my bottle and even put things on it to repulse me, like hair and dirt. Pardon the pun but that sucks. She said I would just brush off any foreign material and then I would enjoy my cow juice. She even resorted to putting chili on the nipple of my bottle. She said she felt bad when she heard me crying as I told my older brothers, "Papo, Kiki ma ma chi chi." This means "Raymond, Richard, taste my bottle." I'm not sure when she finally weaned me, but I'm certain it was before my voice changed (LOL).

My mother knew it was time for me to move on to solid food so I could grow into my next chapter in life. It is much like a new believer in Christ. At first, "You need someone to teach you the elementary words of God's Word.... You need *milk*, not solid food" (Hebrew 5:12). Then as you gain understanding through the straight path of God's word, it is the beginning of wisdom... then you can share and teach others.

As I grew up in the late 1950s, I can remember the first time I was finally old enough to accompany my father and two brothers to the dump (landfill). My father's primary job was at the City of Phoenix collecting trash from alleys. As I always told my friends back then, he does not pick up garbage from trash cans. His job was to pick up large items like water heaters and ramas (tree branches). My father would find small treasures like pre-used hot wheels cars and put them in his lunch box for me. His nickname for me back then was BB gun. He would call me over by saying, "Ven paca BB gun." He would hug me and then mess up my hair. My father was always looking for ways to make extra money for our family. He would sell scrap metal and copper to the junk yard across the street from Jackson school. I distinctly remember the toxic smell as he burned off the covering off of electrical wiring as required by the scrap yard. I used to get mesmerized by the various colors the flames made as the covering on the cobre (copper) melted in the fire. We nicknamed him Scrappy, and I always admired his work ethic and his ability to make extra money by doing handyman jobs.

When we arrived that first time I went to the dump, I was fascinated by all the things that were piled up and wanted to touch everything. The dump had its own special kind of smell, kind of like a mixture of wet pooch (dog) and smashed germs. The stench intensified when the bulldozer stirred things up by moving the pile. It was a challenge for me to walk on the unstirred portions of new trash as they were loose and unstable.

On this first visit, my father told me to go look inside a medium-sized, rectangular box that was close by.

I said, "Huh? Which one? The white one?"

My father responded, "Yeah, that one!" in Spanish.

My oldest brother Papo (Raymond) encouraged me to do it, while my other brother Richard mumbled, "I wouldn't do that if I were you."

I hurried to the box and opened it; my six-year-old eyes were shocked to see a bloody, dead dog inside of it. It was full of maggots and it really scared the heck out of me. My father held his stomach and nearly fell from laughing so hard. It crushed my young spirit, and I was reluctant to investigate any box at this point and just wanted to go home. My father was a practical joker just like his father was.

A cheerful heart is good medicine, but a crushed spirit dries up the bones.

(PROVERBS 17:22)

Going to the dump was an experience I will always remember. Seeing the dead dog showed me that life is full of surprises and not everything is as it appears to be. The dump was full of medium-sized white boxes like the one I opened. The contents of these boxes are dead dogs and they eventually become dry bones. Please take time to read the story in the Book of Ezekiel Chapter 37, the Valley of the Dry Bones. The Lord promises to restore dry bones that are lying on the floor of the valley. What are your dry bones? Is it a loss of job or spouse? Perhaps an injury or bad business deal has left you cynical. Maybe a job promotion that you did not get. What has taken the life out of you? Read and trust in the promise below.

Dry bones, hear the word of the Lord! This is what the Sovereign Lord says to these bones: I will make breath enter you and you will come to life…. Then you will know that I am the Lord.

(EZEKIEL 37: 4–6)

We lived in a small house that had an even smaller shack on our same property lot. My parents rented the small, one-room unit to a young couple named Alice and Sada. They were a newlywed couple and had a baby boy named Tony. My mother always reminded me not to be a nuisance to them. Sada looked gruff like the Indian warrior named, Wind In His Hair, in the movie *Dances with Wolves*.

Alice was probably in her late teens; she was thin and pale and had long, straight, jet black hair like Cher in her younger days. She was always super nice, and she sometimes gave us Jello. Her ancient old dad would sometimes visit and ask us if we wanted some "yellow." He had a heavy Mexican accent and could not say "jello." We used to call him "don yellow"

(Mr. Yellow), and he playfully chased us and pretended he did not like his nickname.

I played a trick on Alice once by knocking on her door and telling her I had found a severed finger in the alley behind our house. Prior to knocking on the door, I rigged a small jewelry box that had cotton inside of it and poked a hole through the bottom of the box. It looked authentic when she took the lid off the jewelry box and saw my middle finger laying in rest covered with a little ketchup for blood. Poor Alice nearly fainted and then screamed when she saw what looked like a cutoff bloody finger.

She shrieked, "Donde, donde lo hallaste?" (where, where did you find it).

When my mother heard all the commotion, she came running to see what was going on. I ended up getting a whipping with a belt from my mom for that prank. Later that same day, I had to apologize to Alice and promise her I would never do anything like that again. Her husband Sada privately told me he thought it was a good joke and he patted me on the head, Sada knew our house was cold at night so he gave me a large furniture padding that was used at his job for moving furniture. It was brand-new and still wrapped in plastic. This ended up being my blanket for most of my youth. (More on this in chapter 17)

As fathers, it is so important to lead your family by example. My grandfather was a practical joker and so was my father. As it says in the Book of John 5:19, Jesus *gave them this answer*: "Very truly I tell you, the Son can only do what he sees his Father doing, because whatever the Father does the Son also does."

Next door to the east of us, there lived an old woman named Mrs. Cox. She looked like a larger and older version of Aunt Bea from the Andy Griffith television show. She used to sing to me a catchy tune named, "Rubin, Rubin, I've been thinking." Her blue eyes would light up and twinkle as she sang. I recently did a search on Google, and I learned this was a jump rope song created in 1871. It can be found under American Children's Songs at www.mamalisa.com. The lyrics went, "Rubin, Rubin I've been thinking, what a strange world this would be. If the boys were all transported far beyond the northern sea." My brother Papo would always encourage her to sing it to us. I'm sure it was a song she jumped rope to as a little girl in the early 1900s.

We spent many summer evenings with Mrs. Cox swinging on her A-frame swing set. Life was simple—we were poor but had everything we needed. Mrs. Cox would ask us to rake her yard, and when we were almost finished, she let my brothers and I know we were not getting paid. She would say, "You know you are doing this for love and not money." When we finished, she demanded a hug from us. I did not like hugging Mrs. Cox because she smothered me in her softness and smelled like an old lady. Papo used to hate it when he heard we were not getting paid and she wanted a hug. He told me he wanted to slug her, not hug her. Mrs. Cox used to tell me stories about how she loved the Lord, but I did not understand what she was talking about. She planted some of my first faith seed into me. This was good because Faith comes from hearing the Word of God. "Consequently, faith comes from hearing the message, and the message is heard through the word about Christ" (Romans 10:17).

The more I think about Mrs. Cox, the more I realize how important it is to remember traditions and to respect our elders. First, we must remember where we have been through stories and traditions; this will guide us to where we are going. Hopefully it is on a path to Wisdom. As taught to children many, many generations ago in the Book of Deuteronomy 6:5–9:

"Love the Lord your God with all your heart and with all your soul and with all your strength. These commandments that I give you today are to be on your hearts. Impress them on your children. Talk about them when you sit at home and when you walk along the road, when you lie down and when you get up. Tie them as symbols on your hands and bind them on your foreheads. Write them down on the door frames of your houses and on your gates."

We can learn so much from individuals that have already lived six to nine decades. The sharing of their life experiences can help guide us while we continue our stepping into Wisdom as we age. Here are just a couple of references about respecting our elders: "is not **wisdom** found among the aged? Does not long life bring understanding?" (Job 12:12) and "For through **wisdom** your days will be many and years will be added to your life" (Proverbs 9:11).

Barrio lesson # 2 You never know what you will find inside a box at the dump.

CHAPTER 3

EARLY BEGINNINGS

In the beginning was the Word, and the Word was with God... The Word became flesh and made his dwelling among us. We have seen his glory, the glory of the one and only Son, who came from the Father, full of grace and truth.

From the Book of John Chapter 1 Verses 1 and 14

At a recent Writers' Conference, the host pastor kicked off the training from the Book of Genesis with the very first verse in the Bible, "In the beginning God made the heavens and the earth." My first thought as my soul gave an undetected sigh was how this is going to connect to the writing conference. I thought to myself, this is going to be a long day. The pastor went on to say God created everything from nothing with words to command things into existence. God said, "Let there be light!", and just like that, there was light for the earth that had been formless and empty. The pastor continued... on the sixth day, God created mankind in his own image. The pastor then said something that made my ears perk up. The pastor made a comparison between God and writers as writers use words to create a little world of their own inside of the book they are writing. How about that! The paradigm shift I received from these words brought any trace of sleepiness to a screeching halt. This insignificant barrio boy had just received a whopping dose of encouragement. Now my spirit has been renewed so I can create my miniature world—this book I have been writing for about three years. My hope is to encourage and enlighten others toward wisdom for God's glory.

Writing this book is risky for me because I openly and freely share my thoughts, experiences, and ideas, and I know this leaves me wide open for the critics. However, it is worth the gamble that if it helps one person, then, without any reservation, it was worth my leap of faith. It is so important for all of us to offer words of encouragement to each other at every opportunity. After all, it does say in Proverbs 18:21, "The tongue has the power of life and death." Choose your words carefully to lead, inspire, and affirm others especially the ones you share life with.

****

At this point it is important for me to fast-forward beyond the barrio walk so I can share my experience of when I became a new creation, a follower of Jesus Christ. I had only known my future wife for a week when she invited me to her church. She was part of the praise team and when I heard her singing, it was like candy for my ears. First, I must mention, I struggled with the thought of attending a Baptist Church. Growing up Catholic, it was not an option to visit another denomination. When I first arrived at the church, I wondered if I would be excommunicated from the Catholic Church. Then I thought, wait a minute, I haven't attended church for almost eight years. So, I took my step out of the boat like Peter, only I could not see Jesus... *yet.*

My decision to accept the Lord as my personal Savior happened on November 13, 1999, at Primera Baptist Church in Fort Worth, TX. This was now my third visit. I liked the way people prayed from their heart and there was always a powerful teaching based on scripture. After a strong message, I thought to myself, if God can use a talking donkey from the story of Balaam found in the Book of Numbers Chapter 22 to further His Kingdom, *He can use me.* The interim pastor stated if anyone wanted to decide to let Christ be the ruler of their life to please raise their hand. I raised my right hand, but he did not see me and continued to lead us in prayer. Following his lead, I sincerely asked Jesus to come into my heart and forgive me of all my sins. So, at age forty-seven, I repented of my sins and, by faith, accepted Christ as my Lord and Savior that crisp November morning. Immediately a rushing wave of warmth, peace, and love seemed to cover me from head to toe and I began sweating profusely. It seemed like a 100-pound weight was taken off my shoulders. Wow! I felt like I was twenty years younger, and in spiritual reality, I was because the old was gone and now I was a new creation. Blow the party horns because the angels were celebrating in Heaven. In Luke 15:7, it reads: "I tell you in the same way there will be more rejoicing in heaven over one sinner who repents than over nine-ty-nine persons who do not need to repent."

My girlfriend then, and now my wife of nineteen years, looked at me sweating and asked, "Are you ok?"

I smiled and whispered, "Oh yes! I'll tell you about it in a while."

After the service, I told her about my experience. She was skeptical as this was only the third service I had ever attended outside of a Catholic Church. She told me later she thought I was only trying to impress her. I had earlier tried to amaze her by putting an entire twenty-dollar bill into the offering container as it passed in front of us.

Back then, I lived in Little Rock and it was a long drive home from Fort Worth where my future wife lived. That night I got home exhausted from my salvation experience and the five-and-a-half-hour drive. I did not pass go and went straight to bed. As I laid down, it felt like I was coming down with a flu and my dry throat was closing faster than a snapping turtle. Under the covers, I was freezing and had chills. As I shivered, I prayed for God to remove whatever illness was invading my body. This was one of my first prayers other than the Our

Father or Hail Mary. God in His goodness and mercy answered me. It felt like something physically wiped my throat with a soft but firm touch. Immediately, there was the feeling again, the wave of warmth, peace, and love, that covered me from head to toe and I began to sweat. It was awesome to feel the healing hand of God! The new creation in Christ fell fast asleep and woke up refreshed without any sign of illness. "Therefore, if anyone is in Christ, the new creation has come: The old has gone, the new is here" (2 Corinthians 5:17).

No matter what you are going through, the healing hand of God can heal you too. He loves you and can take away anything you may be suffering from with one touch. It could be illness, loneliness, shame, guilt, or depression—He can take it away immediately.

In my early beginnings as a born again Christian, I had to abandon using profanity. I remember telling my fiancé, "I need to use some strong language to get their attention, but I don't really mean it." I was referring to getting the mail moved over the telephone when giving out instructions to subordinate managers. It was somewhat of a struggle to stop drinking, and I tested my fiancé by saying, "Don't worry about me drinking, I know how to handle my alcohol." God was good to me and helped me eliminate this vice after thirty years of continuous consumption. Ironically, my last episode of serious drinking was with my underage (for drinking) son Michael a couple of months earlier. We went to Memphis Beale Street and we had more than enough; he was nineteen years old and attending Santa Clara University at that time.

Note to Michael: Always bloom wherever you are planted. Be the reason someone smiles TODAY. I am proud of you and love you unconditionally. Wishing you a lifetime of health and happiness. My prayer is that your home will always be filled with Love, Peace and Joy. Long live the M & M boys!

During my Sunday school lessons for New Believers, I was instructed that it was imperative for me to read the Bible every day, so I bought my first bible. After struggling with "reading the Bible every day" and not knowing on how to begin, I sighed and gave a mental eye roll. I had my Gideon moment and I prayed something like this: "Dear God, if you are real and your word is true, show me some proof." I continued this prayer by saying, "When I open my new bible for the first time and touch whatever verse I land on, show me something that will increase my faith." What happened next has led me to read my bible *every* day for the past 19+ years.

When I opened my bible, my finger landed on Hebrews 4:12. It says, "The word of God is alive and active. Sharper than any double-edged sword, it penetrates even to dividing soul and spirit, joints and marrow, it judges the thoughts and attitudes of the heart." I was stunned and cried for nearly an hour as I knew this was not a coincidence but God caring enough for me to take me to this powerful verse. This was the first time in my life I felt oily tears flowing from my eyes. These tears seemed to cleanse my soul of all skepticism and disbelief. Hmm, here's a thought: If the eyes are a window to our soul, then perhaps our tears serve as binoculars to see into heaven.

Reading in the good book made me re-examine my beliefs. I was upset with some of what I had been taught in 1966. One of the first teachings at the seminary (more on this later) was to pray the novena prayer on the back of a small card with a picture of the founding saint on the front. I was taught if I said this prayer for nine first Fridays and received communion, this **guaranteed** my admission to Heaven. I hope whoever reads this can understand how ludicrous and off base this is.

Here is a list of what I believe (this paraphrases a song called "We Believe" by Newsboys):

1. I believe in God the Father.
2. I believe in Jesus Christ.
3. I believe in the Holy Spirit and He's given us new life.
4. I believe in the crucifixion.
5. I believe Jesus conquered death.
6. I believe in the resurrection and He's coming back again.

I also believe in the verse found in Romans 10:13, "Everyone who calls on the name of the Lord will be saved." God loves us all the same and wants us to spend eternity with him. God examines the heart of every sinner, no matter what the sin is, and grants forgiveness to anyone who sincerely asks for it.

Here are some of the things I had to stop believing as I did not find them in the Bible:

7. There is no purgatory.
8. Mary is not seated at the left hand of the Father. I honor her as Jesus' mother, but she was human. I did not find anywhere that she was given the position as sitting at the left hand of the Father after her assumption (did not find it) into Heaven.
9. You do not have to go to a priest to confess your sins. "There is one God and one Mediator between God and man, the man Christ Jesus" (1 Timothy 2:5).
10. Praying to statues and saints, reciting novenas, and rubbing beads or buddhas will not get you into Heaven. Jesus said it himself: "I am the Way, the Truth and the Life, no one comes to the Father except through me" (John 14:3).

I had to let you as the reader know why I believe like I do so I can continue with this book. This is not to say I am right and you are wrong. Please examine your bible and see for yourself what it says and what it doesn't say.

****

My early beginnings at Jackson school kindergarten were confusing due to my limited vocabulary to speak English. Back home our first and primary language was Spanish. My two older brothers had already been in school for a few years, so I picked up some English from them but not enough to carry on a conversation. I was stunned when I could not understand a single word Miss Lane was speaking. After my first day in kindergarten, I felt like the individuals building the tower of Babel. One day there was perfect communication and then God confused their language. (This story can be found in Genesis 11:8–9.) The teacher paired me up with a girl named Lala that lived a block away from me. She was fluent in English and Spanish. We walked to and from school every day. She even gave me my first kiss brought on by a double dog dare, but that experience is for another story.

Once on my walk home with Lala, some kids began throwing rocks at us. Lala got struck on the knee, and it made me furious. I ran over the railroad tracks to get some rocks and tripped. My left hand still has a small scar from a piece of glass I landed on when I fell. The other kids laughed, and I went berserk, like a broken rock throwing machine that went completely haywire. The other kids never got hit by any of the rocks that I threw, but they quickly left as they saw my fury. I walked Lala, who was crying, all the way to her house and told her mother what had happened. Her mother thanked me for taking care of her and sent me home with a couple of cookies. We were never bothered by those kids again on our daily walks to and from kindergarten.

Going to school introduced me to diversity. There were now kids with "yellow hair," some had freckles, some were white, while others were black. There were also some Native American kids, and I even learned on how to count to five in German from the kids from another state. Diversity in people is like a mosaic masterpiece that God created for us. It would be boring if we all looked the same and ate the same cuisine. I am blessed to love all types of food from so many other countries. Ironically, I do not like the taste of American cheese.

Note to Irma: Always remember the first poem we wrote together twenty years ago. The poem ended up being a song I sang at our wedding. Here are a couple of lines from it:

At the end of the day we'll whistle a tune.

Go to bed with a smile after looking at the moon.

Laughing like children til our faces hurt.

Forever and ever, My Love.

Thank you for being you; I will always love you. Like we say almost every night before going to sleep: "If I don't see you in the morning, I'll see you up there."

Our first date at Rangers vs Yankees in October 1999.
The Rangers lost but we won.

Jackson School Days - 1957

Barrio lesson # 3 Diversity in people is a gift from God.

CHAPTER 4

THE DAY THE TRUMPET DIED

We moved to our house on Sherman Street prior to my beginning kindergarten. It was my home all the way until I left for the Navy. In going to school, I was fortunate to have three older cousins and two brothers at Jackson School. My three cousins, Virgie, Esperanza, and Manuel, lived with us temporarily because their mother had died of cancer. There were nine of us living in a two-bedroom house with one bathroom. We always had enough and over-blessed with love. My cousin Manuel (RIP) had polio, but that never slowed him down or affected his positive attitude. The walks to school were long, and on cold mornings, I had to protect my protruding ears from my siblings and cousin as they like to thump them with their middle fingers as they ran past me. Sometimes on our way to school when it was cold, you could find ice over a shallow puddle of water. I loved to break the ice by stepping hard on it until one day I stepped on a pothole and my foot went through the ice, into the puddle all the way to my ankle. It took all day for my shoe to dry, and it was uncomfortable to go without a sock on my right foot. My brothers and I used to like to pretend like it was not cold, and we strutted with our chest out like the cold had no effect on us. We would yell and repeat, "It ain't cold!" several times as we strolled to school. We would then scream, "It is cold!" and take off running while laughing.

We loved to put things like pennies on the railroad track so they could be flattened by the passing train. Sometimes the pennies ended up several yards away, and if you picked them up too soon, the heat from the smashed "Abe Lincoln" would burn your fingers. We were always warned by our parents to keep our distance from the passing train. As we got older, we learned to jump on the slow-moving flat cars and ride the tracks. The key to getting off was to jump off before the train moved too fast. There was one occasion when my friend Ross was too scared to jump. We yelled "Jump" several times and then sadly waved to him as the train sped away. We got in trouble that day because his father had to drive all the way to Casa Grande (forty-nine miles south of Phoenix or forty-two miles as the crow flies) to pick him up. Ross was one of my closest friends; rest in peace, my brother. "A friend loves at all times, and a brother is born for a time of adversity" (Proverbs 17:17).

My brother Papo was being forced by our parents to play the trumpet. My parents had to rent an expensive trumpet so he could be part of the school marching band and fulfill their dreams that maybe one day he would become a mariachi. Since my brother despised the trumpet, he took care of things his way by putting the trumpet on the railroad tracks just before the train passed. The trumpet and case looked like they had been hit by a meteor as the remains were twisted like a deformed pretzel. As a result, I did not get to learn to play an instrument during grammar school even though my heart's desire was to learn how to play the saxophone. I guess a younger brother is just as guilty if they happen to be there at the scene of the trumpet murder.

We used to have school assemblies and the whole school would gather on the blacktop. One day, a magician entertained us with some slight of hand. Toward the end of his act, he picked out my brother Richard from the crowd and asked him to come onto the stage. My brother was in the second or third grade and was shy and kind of chubby. The magician asked my brother what he had for breakfast.

My brother blurted out, "Oatmeal!"

The magician yelled out, "No you didn't! You had weenies!"

He quickly reached into my brother's shirt and pulled out a string of wieners. It was outrageous and the whole school roared in laughter. I remember asking my brother later if he felt the weenies inside his shirt before he went on stage; what a mystery it was to me.

Did you know there were magicians mentioned in the Bible? It happened during the time when Moses was trying to convince the Pharaoh of Egypt to release the Israelites from slavery. When Pharaoh asked Moses and his brother Aaron to perform a miracle, "Aaron threw down his staff in front of Pharaoh and his officials and it became a snake Pharaoh then summoned wise men and sorcerers, and the Egyptian magicians did the same things by their secret arts: Each one threw down his staff and it became a snake. But Aaron's staff swallowed up their staffs." Now that's an impressive magic show found in the Book of Exodus Chapter 7.

On 19th Avenue there was a small irrigation ditch between Lincoln and Grant streets. It was normally about five- to six-feet wide, but the width of water varied after heavy rainfall. Some of the black kids, we called them colored back then, would cross 19th Avenue and run at full speed to broad jump across the ditch. I never tried it, but it was impressive to watch. Part of the challenge was to time the run in between moving vehicles. My friend nicknamed Houstee was the best at this version of the barrio broad jump. He was a naturally gifted athlete that seemed to have no fear.

I've heard the word fear is mentioned 365 times in the Bible; I haven't counted them. Perhaps fear is mentioned 365 times for each day of the year. After all, "The fear of the Lord is the beginning of knowledge, but fools despise wisdom and instruction" (Proverbs 1:7). The word fear in this context is not like the Lord is the boogie man. Fear, as mentioned in this verse, has to do more with respect, awe, trust, and surrendering control.

Here's a nugget I want to share with you that changed my perspective about the fear of the Lord. It was after one of my moments when I had succeeded at something at my job and received a sizeable windfall. I went for a walk and an ant crossed my path; in my arrogance I thought I *am* to this ant like God is to me and could kill it if I wanted to. Immediately, my inner voice yelled, "You are not even a grain of sand at the bottom of the Indian Ocean compared to I *am*!" What a revelation and humbling experience I received that day. Thank you for this lesson Heavenly Father.

I learned a lot from my black friends like teamwork and competition in any game you played. One of the lessons I learned early on was not to keep any coins in your pocket. Some of the aggressive black kids tapped my pockets, and if they felt any coins, I was pressured to buy them something or share the coins. When I would see them, one of the first things I did was to tap their pocket first. Some of the "your mama" put-downs that were said back then were vicious. My friend "Seesaw" once told another black kid, "Your momma is so fat that if she steps on a dollar bill, it will turn into change!" They would put each other down by saying "Forget you!" The response was, "Forgot you!", followed by, "Never thought about you!" The final response was, "You're forgotten, dead and rotten, be my slave and pick my cotton!" Those were harsh words for schoolboys in the early 1960s.

My brother Papo had an Indian friend named Dennis and they called each other "fool." One day I made the mistake of thinking Dennis' older brother was Papo's friend. I yelled out, "Hey fool!" The older brother looked just like Dennis, and both could have passed as Danny (Machete) Trejo's sons. The older brother was mean and liked to drink from a brown bag. He chased me from Circle K all the way to my house. The real fool, Papo's friend Dennis, thought it was hilarious when I told him about it. He told me his brother was crazy and carried a huge knife. From that day forward, I knew I had to be more careful not to make that mistake again. I made a mental note to respect him and call him Mr. Fool next time. Luckily for me, I never got close enough to Fool's older brother so he could catch me. I once asked Dennis about his brother, and he told me, "He's not a bad guy but some days he just gets up on the wrong side of the teepee."

There are so many ways to get into trouble as you are growing up. Back in the late1950s, any adult could reprimand any child and it kept us kids in check. Teachers could paddle you and so could your aunt, uncle, or babysitter. Once a teacher from another grade pulled my ear and hit me in the back because I reentered the classroom before recess was over.

During those early school years, it seemed like time used to just creep by like a snail still learning to crawl. Now, the days all speed by like a runaway train. As I reflect on how my life has changed, I sometimes wonder where I would be now without the love of Christ. My drinking would have continued, and my health would have deteriorated. I would have continued life without the blessed assurance of knowing where I will spend eternity. My life before Christ had no sense of purpose or direction. I'm sure I would have missed out on blessings and being able to help or care about helping others during the last twenty years. I know what love is, and I also know what love isn't. In 1 John 3:16 it says, "This is how we know what love is: Jesus Christ laid down his life for us. And we ought to lay down our lives for our brothers and sisters."

Professional wrestlers came to our school, and they showed us how to use leverage to flip over another person who was rushing you. Tito Montez and Pancho Pico came to Jackson school with their glittery jackets. Note: Pancho Pico was my father's favorite wrestler, and he would yell, "Picale! Pico!" (sting him Pico) when he watched him wrestle. It was like meeting celebrities at our school that day because we had just seen them on television on live wrestling.

I used to love to go to the Phoenix Madison Square Garden located on 7th Avenue and Jefferson with my father, Tio Mike, cousins, and brothers. There was nearly a riot after the main event when the Mexican wrestler finally won the Arizona State Championship. There was a thunderous celebration when they raised the new champion's hand in victory. Almost immediately, the defeated wrestler named Sputnik Monroe hit the new champ El Gran Lotario with the trophy and split his forehead wide open. There was blood everywhere. My uncle Mike was super enraged. He tried with all his might to get into the ring to get his hands on Sputnik. I remember, my uncle muttering, "I'm gonna get that SOB!" We urged him on by yelling, "Get him Tio!" and my cousins yelled, "Get him dad!"

Luckily, he was not able to get into the ring and narrowly dodged a size 12 kick from Monroe that struck another man and knocked off his glasses. The wrestling may have been staged, but the pandemonium caused afterward by rabid fans sure wasn't. Several city police officers rushed in to disperse the crowd and escort Monroe back to the dressing room.

Growing up one must learn personal responsibility, to respect others, do their best, and follow the rules while perfecting their skills in whatever they choose to do. Once a person figures out what they want to do, then they should put all their heart and passion into it and enjoy the short time we are here on earth. I strongly urge everyone to read your B.I.B.L.E. as this stands for **b**asic **i**nstructions **b**efore **l**eaving **e**arth.

Keep this in mind: "Remember your Creator in the days of your youth, before the days of trouble come and the years approach you when you will say, 'I find no pleasure in them'" (*Ecclesiastes 12:1*).

Barrio Lesson # 4: Never put a rented musical instrument on the railroad track when the train is about to pass by.

CHAPTER 5

CELEBRATING CHRISTMAS
IN 1958

We lived in a small two-bedroom house close to the Arizona State Capitol and just south of the tracks. During the winter the weather temperature would sometimes drop below freezing point. Our house did not have central heating, so it was warmed by a fireplace in the living room and the gas stove in the kitchen. I never slept in pajamas because I did not have any, so I slept on in my skivvies (Navy slang for underwear). When you don't have pajamas and have never worn them, you don't miss them because you don't know what it feels like to have them. Our bedroom was about six feet by eight feet, and most of the room was absorbed by a bunk bed. Papo and I slept on the top bed, and Richard slept on the bottom with Lupe. No one liked to sleep with Lupe because she sometimes wet the bed. One of our nightly rituals was to attach a pillowcase to the hook on a fishing pole. Once the lights went off, Papo and I would dangle the pillowcase from the top bunk and make ghost noises. This would scare Lupe and she would cry. We thought it was hilarious to make "the ghost" fly all over the room. Hmm…maybe this is why she wet the bed.

There was a small refrigerator in the kitchen just outside of our bedroom. It had a locking mechanism that closed forcefully. We used to stick things like pencils and Popsicle sticks in it to make them get snapped in half. My brothers always warned me not to put my finger in there and I didn't, but it sure looked tempting. My brother Richard and I raided the fridge early one Easter morning and ate the hard-boiled eggs that had been cooked for the potato salad. We threw the eggshells under the bed and slept peacefully that night. The next day, my mother was upset with us and kept saying, "This potato salad would taste so much better with some hard-boiled eggs." Papo also kept mentioning to her throughout the day how much he liked potato salad with egg as he snickered at us. Our Easter get-togethers provided some fond memories. We would get together with my Tio Joe and Tia Tillie and kids and spend the day at the Estrella Mountain Park. We ran all over those mountains and would only come back to our gathering spot when we got hungry.

It was a blessing to grow up having a strong family foundation. Early on it was my two parents, two older brothers, myself, and one younger sister. My siblings and I were two years apart in age, and then there was a six-year gap and my parents had my two younger sisters and my younger brother born with Down syndrome. My family was close, and they helped to teach me values and unconditional love in a way no one else can. At the same time, there were times when we could disappoint each other. Treasure your parents and siblings because it sure leaves an empty place inside your heart and soul when they go on into eternity. I'm looking forward to having a family reunion when we all meet in Heaven.

* * * *

Not too long ago, my younger brother Ernie, who has Down syndrome, asked me in his own words, "Come on Luben (he has trouble pronouncing the letter R). Tell me the truth, is there really a heaven?" I answered him by paraphrasing from the Book of John Chapter 13 about the day Jesus was saying goodbye to his disciples (I said friends). I went on to tell him Jesus said he was going to his Father's house in heaven to prepare a place for them. Jesus' friend named Thomas was confused and said, "Lord, we don't know where you are going, so how can we know the way?" Jesus answered, "I am the way and the truth and the life. No one comes to the Father except through me" (John 14:5–6). Note to reader: notice how Jesus said *I am the way*. He *did not say I am one of the ways*, this is so important to understand.

I finished by telling my younger brother that Jesus does not lie and He said He was going to heaven. Ernie felt better after hearing this story. I coerced Ernie into praying that day, and after much badgering, he lowered his head and closed his eyes and said, "God bless." I looked up and chuckled and said, "That's it, that's your prayer." Ernie smiled and said, "Yup!" What a profound prayer, he covered it all.

* * * *

My father would go to the nearby lumbar yard to get scrap wood to burn in the fireplace. It gave me a sense of pride to go with him and bring back a truckload of wood so we could keep the family warm. It didn't bother me to get splinters as I helped him load and unload the truck because I knew it would keep us warm. Sometimes we got lucky and a front-end loader would drop the wood remnants onto the back of the truck.

We burned things in the fireplace like newspapers, paper plates, and anything that would add heat to the house. We would make baked potatoes in the fireplace by wrapping aluminum foil around them and placing them in the embers. We also toasted marshmallows by putting them on the end of an extended wire hanger. I made it a point not to leave the wire hangers readily available. My mother sometimes used the extended wire hangers to stop my brothers and I from being disobedient. I probably still have scar tissue on my tongue from biting into the marshmallow too soon. We tried to make some Jiffy Pop once but all it did was make a mess in a jiffy. Those Jiffy Pop makers were fun to watch as the foil expanded as each kernel popped. There wasn't a lot of popcorn, but it was just enough to give everyone a taste. It worked sort of like the time Jesus multiplied the fish and loaves.

One time I threw one of my sister's dolls in the fireplace and thought no one would find out. The darn doll did not cremate the way I thought it would because of the hard plastic it was made from. I was not allowed to play with my friends for two days after the melted doll provided the DNA to convict me of doll destruction. Those types of dolls had a rubber head with fake hair woven in. The dolls' eyes would close when my sister laid it down and open when she picked them up. Most dolls in those days had blue eyes and "yellow" hair. That's the term I used before I learned the word blonde. Oh, that reminds me of the two blondes sitting on the beach in California. One of the blondes asked the other, "Which is further, Florida or the moon?" The other blonde quickly replied, "*Duhhh*! You can't see Florida!"

Oh, I just remembered, this story is about Christmas. Let me tell you about our Christmas tree. It had decorations that we made in school like chain links made from colored paper… it took the place of garland. The tree was dusted with fake spray-on snow that made a mess. I remember the tree having some cylinder lights with colored liquid that bubbled once the base was hot enough. My brothers told me there was Kool-Aid inside the bulb, and I secretly broke one to taste the liquid. Much to my disappointment, there was no flavor in the liquid, and I was lucky not to drink any glass fragments.

It was early Christmas morning when I woke up to the sound of my brother yelling, "Bikes! Bikes!" We ran toward the living room as fast as we could. I remember not making the turn around the stove and went sliding on the vinyl floor into the cabinet doors underneath the sink. I slid because I was wearing my mock socks, that is, short for moccasin socks—we used to call them muck clucks. I bounced off the doors and quickly scrambled to my feet. When I made it into the living room, I saw three beautiful brand-new bicycles. My bike was smaller than my brothers' bikes and it had training wheels. My parents and brothers told me Santa Claus had brought them into the house while we were asleep.

We immediately went outside to test ride our new treasures. I rode mine in front of my beloved Lala's house. I was not there long before her dog chased me away. My little legs peddled with all my terrified strength to get away. As I tilted my bike to make a turn, one of the training wheels lost contact with the ground. It was eery to hear the whirling sound as the training wheel was spinning in the air. Being chased by Cujo was not part of my Christmas morning plan, but I somehow made it home without any missing toes as the dog's snapping teeth were close and frightening.

Sometime before New Year's Day, my nino (godfather) brought me a nice yellow Tonka dump truck. I was only able to enjoy the truck for a couple of hours of moving sand and other material. My jealous brother Papo smashed my new truck with a big rock used as a garden border. I remember screaming at him, "When I'm big and you're little, I will pay you back!" Back then I meant what I said but now have long ago forgiven my brother. It's so important for all of us to get rid of any unforgiveness "For if you forgive other people when they sin against you, your heavenly Father will also forgive you" (Matthew 6:14).

Sidenote: My brother Papo recently was ordained a pastor in a non-denominational church in Phoenix, AZ. He has dedicated his later years to supporting an orphanage in Nogales, Mexico. I sure hope none of those kids receive any yellow Tonka dump trucks (LOL).

During the Christmas break from school, our family went to visit my paternal grandparents who lived in East Los Angeles. The ride in our 1954 Mercury took forever. We must have asked, "Are we there yet?" about fifty times before reaching Wickenburg. Their house sat on top of the biggest hill I had ever seen, and when we came over the top of the hill, it caused a metabolic reaction in my stomach. I immediately had to run into their house and straight to their bathroom—good thing I was wearing my brown pants (just kidding). It was so embarrassing to have to run past my grandparents while unbuckling my pants. Their backyard was full of plants and they had peach and avocado trees. I got to meet my uncles Ralph and Teyo that were full of mischief. They always seemed to have snacks like corn chips and mixed nuts. My uncle Ralph asked me if I like Fritos and I said they were my favorite. He held me down and laughed, and then he took off his shoes and socks and put his "free toes" all over my face. Note: I have carried on the tradition by giving away lots of free toes to my sons, nephews, and now grandsons. My uncles were full of life and had a pool table and makeshift boxing ring in the basement. They got together down there with their homies, and their entertainment was watching some serious late-night "live boxing." It was a rough neighborhood, but you don't notice those things as a young boy.

My other uncle Eliseo and my aunt Alice came over to my grandparents' house; I can remember my cousin Mariam unwrapping a present that had a windup monkey that banged cymbals. That day I met my three girl cousins, Esther (RIP), Conchita, and Mariam and my two male cousins, Boy (Alex) (RIP) and Yaychi (Carlos). We went to my Tio Eliseo's house in La Mirada. Yaychi and I became good buddies. When we heard our dads were going to the store, we begged to go with them. They told us we could not go, but somehow, we managed to sneak into the trunk of the car. My uncle's car had damage in the back from an accident and we could look through a hole in the trunk as they headed to the liquor store. It was fascinating to see the other cars from that viewpoint, but the smell of gas was nauseating. When we got there, we yelled, "Hey! Let us out!" My tio and dad were surprised to see us back there. My father laughed but my uncle said he was going to teach us a lesson when we got home. He never did once they started drinking.

Our Christmas vacation ended up with a trip to Disneyland. It was awesome! Sadly, much like many of my Christmases, the real meaning of Christmas was never celebrated. It is so important to share the Christmas story about our Savior being sent to earth. Make time at your Christmas gathering to read about how Jesus was born in a manger. Talk about that first Christmas in Bethlehem. Sing songs like, "Silent Night" and "Angels we have heard on high." "For God so loved the world that He gave His one and only Son, that whoever believes in him shall not perish but have eternal life" (John 3:16).

My brother "Big Ern" who has taught me so much.

Barrio lesson # 5 Santa Claus is real and does visit the barrio.

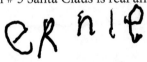

CHAPTER 6

MEANWHILE BACK IN
THIRD GRADE

This year in school was the most memorable of any school year including graduate school at the University of Colorado. The year started with a bang and continued all the way to fourth grade.

My third-grade teacher was tall and lanky; she looked like a mixture of Jane Hathaway from *The Beverly Hillbillies* and the evil witch from *The Wizard of OZ*. On the first day of school, she emphasized we should not lean back on our desk or we would fall. Almost immediately after saying this, she leaned back too far and was a twisted, embarrassed mess as she fell to the floor. She was wearing a dress and my eyes saw more of her than they bargained for. She began to cry as a couple of parents untangled her from the third-grade student-size desk. My friend Rosco and I lost respect for her and we made fun of her at any opportunity. We once spotted her eating baby food as part of her post-surgery meal. We pointed and laughed; she was really agitated that we took away her privacy that day. Rosco was like a brown tornado that stirred up anything around him. He was a bully that made fun of the Navajo kids by yelling "Unga! Bunga!" at them. Rosco's nickname was Gila, short for Gila monster.

Miss Smith was unprofessional and told Rosco and me that we were not worth our salt. I did not understand what she meant by this but have since learned, "If salt loses its saltiness… it is no longer good for anything, except to be thrown out and trampled underfoot" (Matthew 5:13). She also told us we were like wild Indians and would never amount to anything in life.

One day she made the mistake of putting Rosco and me in the cloakroom to paint on a double-sided easel. My painting was of a house with an apple tree in the front yard. I decided to make it rain on my masterpiece by flicking some blue paint at the canvass. As I flicked, Rosco peered around the side and soon had blue freckles. He yelled, "Hey!", and whisked some paint back at me. Almost instantly, we had a full-fledged paint fight in the cloakroom. Miss Smith was furious and paddled us in front of the class. We were indignant and told her it did not hurt. Somehow, she got a splinter in her hand from the paddle and began to cry. She wailed, "Look what you made me do!"

We had to clean the cloakroom, and for additional punishment, she said we had to stay in there while the rest of the class watched a cartoon. We did not obey and when the lights went out, we crawled like army men to a spot where we could enjoy the Popeye cartoon. We threatened the other kids not to tell on us. We were able to caterpillar our way back into the cloakroom undetected just as Popeye finished his can of spinach. As a sidenote, I loved cartoons and somehow had the ability to dream them in color. We only had black-and-white television back then. My brothers did not believe when I described my dreams in color. When she turned the lights back on, she said we could rejoin the class. She asked us if we learned our lesson and with a sly smirk, we said, "Yes! Miss Smith."

My mother went with me to teacher-parent meeting, and Miss Smith was almost unrecognizable with the gobs of makeup she wore that evening. She told my mother I was one of her favorite students, and I wanted to scream, "You lie like a rug!" She acted extra sweet, and later I told my mom she was just faking it and was mean as a yellow jacket wasp. I remember how pretty my mom looked that day, and I felt special to be with her. She seldom wore makeup, and she looked prettier than Mary

Tyler Moore from *The Dick Van Dyke Show*. The year was 1960 and my mother was thirty-two years old.

It seemed like I got into lots of trouble hanging around with Rosco. My mother did not like Rosco's profanity or when he taught me how to flip a bird. She was livid when she read the note from the principal explaining we got detention after school for spitting on other kids. Spitting is one of the most demeaning and disrespectful things you can do to someone. As I wrote this, I thought about Jesus being slapped and spit on by the governor's soldiers from Matthew 27:28–30. I also thought about Jesus crucified on the cross where historians say He was eye level to spectators who wagged their heads and hurled insults. This revelation came to me that brought instant tears to my eyes: *while Jesus was hung on the cross, He was probably spit upon, and the worst part of it, He could not wipe the spit off His face and died with it on Him.*

My mother would tell me a saying, "Dime con quien andas y te diré quien eres." This means, "tell me who you hang around with and I will tell you who you are." I never liked that saying. It is true that "Bad company corrupts good character" (1 Corinthians 15:33). I can almost still hear her say, "A bad piece of fruit can make a good piece of fruit get rotten. The same thing happens to people that hang around with bad friends."

On our way home from school, I once stopped at the Circle K store with a classmate named Lawrence. He wore large square glasses that covered half of his face. He reminded me of a human owl. Occasionally I had some pocket change from collecting the deposit I received for returning glass soda bottles or that my Tio Manuel (mom's brother) gave me. I would use the change to buy some double bubble gum. As we were leaving the store, the attendant called us back. He demanded that Lawrence hand over the Twinkies he had put inside his pants. At first, Lawrence denied he had anything until the attendant threatened to call the police. Lawrence unzipped his trousers and handed over the smashed Twinkies. I could not believe that he had done this.

The attendant told us we could not leave, and he proceeded to call the police. It was difficult for me to understand why I had to stay since I had not stolen anything. I began to cry when the police wrote a report as they interrogated us. They called my mother and she was furious when she got to the store. The police told her I had been detained because I was with someone who had shoplifted. My mother made me apologize to the store attendant and the police officers before we left. It was humiliating and taught me a lesson on being an accomplice. "Walk with the wise and become wise, for a companion of fools suffers harm" (Proverbs 13:20).

On the solemn walk home with my mother, I had to hear it again, "Show me who you hang around with and I'll tell you who you are." I told her I was going to beat up Lawrence, and she said, "I better not hear about it!" This was her way of giving implied consent, so the next day I followed Lawrence into the boy's restroom and gave him a serving of street justice. I punched him in the stomach about seven or eight times faster than he could say, "that hurts!" I stopped being friends with "Lawrence of Arabia," his new nickname after that incident. He probably would not have shared the Twinkies anyway if he had gotten away with them.

One day during recess, a kid from the fifth grade told Rosco and me he wanted to show us a trick but we would have to follow his instructions. He told us to kneel on the blacktop and then take three huge breaths and hold it. He then told us to put our thumb in our mouth and blow out hard without letting any air escape. Rosco passed out instantly and his head hit the blacktop. I did not lose conscientiousness because when I saw Rosco go down, I gasped for air. When Rosco raised his head, it looked like someone had implanted a golf ball under the skin on his forehead. It caused a big commotion and the school nurse had to attend to Rosco. Miss Smith blamed me for Rosco's concussion. By this time in the school year, she knew paddling did not work on me, so she put me in to corner of the room. She made me place my nose about an inch from the wall and told me I better not turn around. It was difficult for me to be still as it felt so confining and staying still was not part of my nature.

Many times, when we want something to happen, it seems confining and it is so hard to wait on God's answer. I'm glad His plans are always better than mine as I have learned to be more patient. One of my favorite bible verses is "Be still and know that I am God." It is God's way of reminding me He has a plan for my life and He who began a good work in me will carry it on to completion until the day of Christ Jesus.

There was a time during the school year I had to read aloud in front of the class. I was reading about the red-winged black bird. Miss Smith told me to try to make the sound of the bird as I read. I continued reading and said the bird made a noise that went, "Caw! Caw! Caw!" Miss Smith told my classmates to close their eyes as I read so they could imagine a red-winged black bird. She made me read it a couple of times, and some of the kids would later tease me by going "Caw! Caw! Caw!" when I walked by. I think it was Miss Smith's way of getting back at me.

One of the things that really annoyed me about Miss Smith happened shortly before Christmas break. She showed us a beautiful Christmas ornament that she was going to give away as a prize. Even though the ornament would not look good on our aluminum Christmas tree, I was determined to win. Our tree came with a light stand and color wheel that rotated in front of the light to make the tree change colors. Anyway, Miss Smith said, "The first student that spells the six-letter word beginning with the letter T and is something people eat during Christmas gets the ornament."

I quickly wrote out t-a-m-a-l-e and nearly ran to give it to her. I thought for sure I had the winning answer, but she said, "Nope." Another student walked up with the answer turkey and Miss Smith handed over the ornament. I'm still disappointed Miss Smith did not understand cultural diversity, and as far as I am concerned, she was a big turkey that day.

God bless you Miss Smith for making my third-grade school year so memorable.

Barrio lesson # 6 Find the right people to hang around with.

CHAPTER 7

INNOCENCE SHATTERED

A s a young boy, I loved to spend the day at my Tio's house in South
Phoenix. At that point, my tios had five sons and one daughter; they
went on to have another three girls to complete their nest of kids. They
lived near areas that had farming, so we got to explore cornfields and
swim in the canalitos (irrigation canals). We had numerous adventures
as we were a gang of eight rowdy boys having good old-fashioned fun
without the Internet, Facebook, video games, or cell phones. Our families
were poor, but we had everything we needed and ate simple food like
beans, fideos, and tortillas. We were blessed with food commodities like
powdered milk, blocks of cheese, and big cans of processed meat that
tasted like Spam. "Blessed are the poor in spirit, for theirs is the kingdom
of heaven" (Matthew 5:3).

My tios were full of life and I remember one of their neighbors could
not say Aurora, so she called my aunt Miss Dora. Tio Mike and Miss Dora
used to like to sing the song "You Are My Sunshine"; they harmonized
well. One of my memories of their house was they had a television that was
connected to a coin box. In order to watch television, you had to deposit
a quarter. I guess this was "good old days" version of pay-per-view. It was
someone's marketing brainstorm of being able to pay for the television as
it was watched. Each quarter kept the television on for an allotted set of

time; then it would turn off when the time expired. It usually happened at critical times like during *The Wizard of OZ*. As we looked frantically for a quarter, we missed part of the flying monkey scene but had the meter back on with enough time to see the witch melt.

My uncle raised chickens and we would catch them and throw them up onto the telephone wires. My uncle would come outside and pretend he could not see his trembling chickens holding on for dear life to the telephone wire. He would say, "Where are my chickens?" We would giggle and shrug our shoulders. The chickens were chicken to let go of the telephone wire, so we had to coax them off with baseballs and baseball gloves. We used to hypnotize the chickens by holding them down, petting them, and tracing circles with a stick around them. The chicken's eyes would close, and you could see their eyeballs move upward inside their saggy eyelids. Once we knew they were asleep, we would slap them awake. I know it sounds cruel, but we never really hurt the yard birds. Please understand, we were in the barrio and this was during my BC (before Christ) years. Once I committed my life to be a follower of Jesus, he removed my heart of stone and gave me a heart of flesh (Ezekiel 36:26).

Another one of our mean boy tricks was to catch a large bumblebee inside the blossom by shutting the flower quickly while the bee was busy gathering pollen. We would break the flower near the top of the stem. We would then shake the flower and run as we released the agitated bumblebee. During those times, I never got stung and have remained fearless of flying insects. In my lifetime, I have been stung by yellow jackets about five or six times. My cousin nicknamed Manny Moose got stung by a yellow jacket right under his eye. That day we were throwing rocks at a palm tree that caught our baseball and disrupted our game. That baseball is probably still stuck in that palm tree in Alkire Park, which sits diagonally across from Our Lady of Fatima Church.

Alkire Park had a public swimming pool that was full of kids and chaos during those hot summer days in Phoenix. The black kids used to hold me underwater, and at first it was terrifying. I had to learn to relax by going limp while underwater, and they would let me go as I confused them like I was no longer breathing. All things work for the good, and in my older years, I have no fear of water and have been blessed to see the magnificent colors God has for us in the beautiful Caribbean. I used to terrorize black kids smaller than me at Alkire Park by giving them lessons on how to snorkel without a snorkel.

We (brothers and cousins) were fascinated by flying insects. We would catch cicadas and tie a thread around them so we could watch them fly in circles above our head as we held the thread. You had to be careful not to tie the thread too tightly or you could cut the big-eyed bug in half. As kids we were told that if you put a live cicada in your mouth, you would be able to yell louder when it flew out. It was somewhat gross to do, but we tried it and yelled as loud as we could when it flew out. Hmm… I'll have to share this with my grandkids while they are still naive enough to try it. I'll also mention, if they want to grow a thick mustache, it will grow best by rubbing fresh-cut garlic under their nose.

One of my younger cousins once stepped on a board that had a large nail protruding from it. The nail went completely through an area near the top of his big toe on his bare foot. It was gruesome to see, and it hurt my ears to hear him scream as he was stuck to the board. His oldest brother, Big Q, quickly straddled the board and dislodged Totoli (RIP) by pulling him straight up. I'm sure it hurt him but nothing like what Jesus felt when large nails were driven into his hands and feet during His crucifixion.

We were lucky to come out of our childhood without any life-altering injuries. My other cousin, closest to my age, once found a 22-caliber bullet and struck it with a hammer. The bullet found its resting place in one of his ankles. My cousin Baby Saw (RIP) was probably the rowdiest of the bunch. He loved to gather used car tires into a pile and then set them on fire. Burning rubber tires sent off a dark black cloud of smoke. We would always scatter when we heard the fire truck sirens getting closer. We would then arrive at the scene as spectators so we could watch the firefighters make the black smoke turn gray and then stop.

My brothers would make me do things to prove my worthiness if I wanted to hang around with them. They had me go into large irrigation pipes under streets and I had to come out on the opposite side. I suffered with tunnel phobia for most of my adult life as a result. Sometimes I was not able to make it to the other side because there were curves in the pipes. When this happened, it caused instant panic in me because it was so dark. I would talk to myself down there to stop the panic attack that came from being semi-entombed. For whatever reason, it was comforting to smell my small, sweaty hand, and it somehow connected me back to my senses to hurry up and get out of there. The tunnels with curves had no room to turn around, so when I had to back up, it was without the aid of that beeping noise large trucks make (LOL). I would come out of the tunnel wide-eyed and clammy. My brothers would dust me off to make sure I did not have any spiders, centipedes, or scorpions attached to me.

I got even with my older cousins and brothers once by hiding in the cornfields. I laid down several rows away from where they were and stayed completely quiet. I chuckled as they looked and called for me for about a good half hour. Note: Later in life I would get anxiety attacks when I had to drive through a tunnel. Somehow it felt like my vehicle was going down the drain. The verse from 2 Timothy 1:7 repeated over and over cured me of my tunnel phobia. It goes like this: "God didn't give us a spirit of fear, but of power and love and a sound mind."

Our parents and tios would sometimes take all of us to the drive-in and we would make our own popcorn at home before the show. The giant size portion of popcorn was gathered into a large grocery bag for all of us to share. Our families were too poor to have butter to put into the popcorn. Baby Saw liked to put a finishing touch on the brown bag by putting cooking oil on the outside of the bag so it "looked like it had butter and tasted good." Baby Saw and my uncle showed me lots of affection whenever we arrived at their house. They called me buddy, and it was a joy to hug them as we said our hellos and goodbyes.

Getting to my main point in this chapter, we had spent a long day at the house of my father's coworker. As kids, we played outside all day, while the adults played cards, smoked cigarettes, and drank beer. My father and his working buddy must have been extra thirsty that day and drank more beer than they should have. They got into a heated argument later that evening, and before we knew it, my brothers, sister, and I were rapidly corralled into the backseat of our 1954 blue and white Mercury. I remember this man challenging my father to a fight by telling him he was not a man if he left without fighting. My mom and the other wife were pleading and pushing my father to get into the car. It was a moment filled with terror, and I could tell something bad was about to happen.

The couple we were visiting just happened to receive fresh milk delivery, so there was an empty milk bottle to be picked up on a container by their fence. Just as we were about to drive away, my dad's coworker grabbed the empty, thick, gallon-size milk bottle and hurled it at the back of our car. It sounded like an explosion when the heavy bottle hit against the back window and shattered it. I felt chunks of glass go down my collared shirt that was tucked into my pants. There were lots of chaos with us four kids screaming and the other wife yelling at her husband and yanking him back inside their house. My mother pulled us out of the car, and I felt embarrassed as she pulled my pants and underwear down to get the squared pieces of glass out of my clothing. I remember shivering and jumping up and down to make sure there was no glass on me. My sister Lupe sustained a deep gash in her elbow; my brothers and I were traumatized but not hurt.

It was hard to accept that someone could do this, and my mother cried angry words against him. This man came over the next day and apologized on his knees. It was many years later that I saw one of this man's sons. I asked him if he remembered the time his father had shattered the back window of the car. He asked me if I knew what had happened to his father the next day. He said my other uncles (dad's brothers) came to their house and dragged his father into their backyard. They proceed to beat the heck out of him and left him on the ground. He told me how much it hurt him to watch his father get knocked around and there was nothing he could do about it. I felt badly for his son as he told me the rest of the story.

This last part of the chapter was difficult to write, even though it is almost sixty years later. I take comfort in knowing, "By His wounds, you have been healed" (1 Peter 2:24). Jesus loved us so much that He bore our sins in His body on the cross so we might die to sin and live for righteousness.

Barrio lesson # 7 Drinking too much makes people cray cray.

CHAPTER 8

PAPER PUNKS

Somewhere around the fourth grade, I began to carry the morning newspaper with my two older brothers. My first newspaper drop-off station was at Buck's Market on the corner of 19th Avenue and Hadley. This was not my first means of making money because we hustled and shined shoes in the Phoenix downtown area. We built our own shoeshine boxes and somehow managed to buy shoe polish to go with an old T-shirt for buffing. One of the tricks of the trade was to get your face low near the boots you were shining and make squeaking noises with your mouth. It sounded like a high-pitched series of squeaks that we had previously mastered at home. I remember a tall man wearing black cowboy boots say, "That sounds like a really good shine, boy." He patted me on the head and gave me a quarter for that squeaky, clean shine. Our normal shoeshine price was a dime. *Yes!* During my working life, I have always tried to give my best possible effort. A good model to follow is found in Colossians 3:23, "Whatever you do, work at it with all your heart, as if you are working for God, and not for man."

Being a paperboy was challenging for a nine-year-old boy as we had to get up at 4:30 am to prepare our newspapers for delivery by wrapping a rubber band around them. It was more strenuous on Sundays because on that day, we had to insert the comics and advertisements. During the winter, it was cold, so we wore two pairs of pants and double jackets.

We worked with a pair of twins named Tommy and Ray. Ray's nickname was "Fahtoo" because when he came to our house, he yelled "Fahtoo!" instead of knocking on our door. Ray and Tommy both looked like the Hispanic version of Fat Albert. Both were somewhat corpulent and always hungry. We always called each other paper punks instead of paperboys. I used to like to go to the store with Fahtoo because he could not count change, so he would always buy me something for helping with his transaction.

One morning when Fahtoo arrived at the newspaper station, he was so excited he could barely talk. He stuttered as he told us, "Cah-cah come l-l-look qui-quick! The p-p-pie truck driver got in a wreck and can't get out of his tr-tr truck!" He took us about a block away to the one-vehicle accident scene. He proceeded to jump into the back of the disabled pie truck. Fahtoo was like a human bakery production line as he handed us fresh pies. The helpless pie truck driver, who had a back injury, was moaning as loud as he could, "Help! They're stealing my pies!" We were out of there in a matter of seconds. That morning we had ate a variety of pies for breakfast. We salvaged a couple of pies and hid them in the telephone booth to have after our morning delivery run. We justified our pie pilfering by convincing ourselves that no one would have bought day-old pies that had been involved in a vehicle accident. We laughed and filled our pie holes (old term for mouths) that morning, I'm glad we did not receive a message from Heaven with some writing on the wall.

There is an interesting story in the Book of Daniel Chapter 5. It tells of King Belshazzar hosting a great banquet for his nobles. Belshazzar had given orders to bring gold and silver goblets taken from the temple in Jerusalem. While entertaining his drunken friends, they drank wine from the goblets and praised the gods of gold and silver, bronze, iron, wood, and stone. The king probably thought it was funny, but the laughter surely stopped when a floating hand appeared and wrote on the plaster of the wall. The writing on the wall declared Belshazzar's days were numbered.

Check out the story for yourself, it's a good one. This is where the expression of "seeing the writing on the wall" comes from.

****

Many years later, my brothers and I saw Ray and Tommy at their father's viewing prior to his burial. In front of the casket, Ray said to his brother, "Tommy, se mira bien Pa," which means "Dad looks good." Tommy replied, "Se mira bien muerto," which means, "he looks completely dead." We knew we weren't supposed to, but we had a good laugh during an otherwise somber wake in front of their dad's casket.

****

One of my regular routines after finishing the paper route was to meet my brothers at the Charlen Cafe for breakfast. The waitress would ask us what we wanted for breakfast, and in unison we would yell out, "Cheeseburgers!" The waitress and some of the regular trucker customers would get a kick out of us eating cheeseburgers for breakfast.

There was a laundromat near our paper station and next door to the Charlen Cafe. We would go in there to get warm by going into the large dryers. One of us would insert the necessary coins and close the door after the person who wanted to get warm. Once the dryer started moving, you had to move like a hamster on a wheel so you would not tumble dry. We couldn't stay there very long unless we put socks on our hands.

The laundromat had a vending machine that had a long rectangular glass door where you could see the vertically stacked bottles of various sodas. To get sodas, after you inserted your coins, a lever would release the soda you chose. We just happened to notice you could pull the soda bottle partially out without inserting money. All we had to do then was to take a bottle opener and a cup to help ourselves to some free soda. We would do this in the wee hours so no one would notice. Before too long, the soda machine was replaced by one that opened like an ice chest. The sodas were now lined up on a track and the bottles were standing upright. This was still easy for us to figure out. We already had a bottle opener and the Charlen Cafe had straws. At this point, close your eyes and pretend you hear loud slurping noises.

For some unknown reason, they moved the location of our newspaper station to a gasoline station located on 21st Avenue and Van Buren. It took us longer to get there, so if we were running late, we would "take the freeway" on our bicycles. We would go down the northbound ramp near Jefferson and take the next exit on Adams. We were young and fearless and somehow, through the grace of God, never got any speeding tickets. We used to love to stand on the bridge of the Jefferson overpass and spit on vehicles as they traveled underneath us on the Black Canyon Freeway. It took skill and perfect timing to land three synchronized, brotherly spits on the windshield of a moving vehicle. We thought it was hilarious until one day a trucker doubled back and threatened to clean his windshield with our noses. That incident retired us from our game of freeway spitting.

Note: The Black Canyon Freeway was the first one to be built in Phoenix. One of my school friends named Alberto (RIP) lost his life as he was playing in the construction zone and a wall of dirt collapsed on him. There were areas under construction that had pipes large enough you could ride your bike inside of them. It was probably dangerous to do this, but the opening was there, and we did not know better.

No one knows when their life will end, so it is important to pray: "Teach us to number our days, that we may gain a heart of wisdom" (Psalm 90:12). I had several friends that did not get to finish their barrio walk.

We really weren't bad kids, but we were nowhere close to being saints either. We worked hard to deliver and collect for our newspaper routes. There were times when I would have to go to a house several times to collect what was due. On one occasion, I was with my brothers and we were collecting at a trailer park near 18th Avenue and Buckeye. An old customer named Charlie, probably about as old as I am now, did not want to pay. He was outside of his trailer drinking beer with another man. As we approached and asked to be paid, he yelled, "Git out of here, you lit-tle meskins!" in his Southern drawl. The other man, Paul, who was also our newspaper customer, jumped to his feet and delivered a beautiful one-punch knockout as we cheered and clapped. He pulled out Charlie's wallet from his back pocket and gave us what he owed plus a dollar tip. It ended up being a good day at the office.

One day while I was riding my bicycle to collect in the afternoon, I was headed east on Sherman going toward the Boy's Club. I made a right turn near the stop sign at 17th Avenue directly across from the King's Rest Motel. Another bike happened to be going northbound, and we crashed and both of us fell off our bicycles. We did not get hurt but got up some-what embarrassed. I remember wondering about the chance of being at the same corner at the same precise time to crash into each other. Isn't that how life is sometimes? God puts people in our path who may knock us down or teach us something along the way. If you get knocked down, get up, dust yourself off, and keep riding through your barrio. "The race is not to the swift or the battle to the wise... but time and *chance* happen to all" (*Ecclesiastes 9:11*).

There were times when dogs chased me, and I would sometimes take my dog "Champ" with me to fend off other dogs. Champ was a boxer and was very protective of me. I got in trouble once because Champ went through a screen door to teach a yappy Chihuahua a lesson. There was a lot of commotion that day when Champ busted into their house via the screen on the door. The woman in the house was making tortillas, and her children were watching *The Wallace and Ladmo Show* on television. I had a hard time dragging Champ out of their house. My father had to repair their screen door and the small dog never bothered me again. The man (husband) that owned the house later told me it's about time someone shut that dog up.

Champ was an awesome dog and in my corny style, I would brag about him. I told my friends that Champ could talk. They said, "yeah right." I told them when I ask Champ what his favorite bird is, he'll reply, "Owwll!" If I ask him, "What's on top of the house?" he'll say "Roof!" And finally, if I ask him, "How does it feel when you sit on coarse sandpaper?" he'll reply, "Ruff!" I told you it was corny.

One day my father was going to Moe's Food Fair Market and asked me if I wanted to go with him. That's like asking a mouse if he wants some cheese. He told me Champ would have to stay home. I jumped in the back of the truck, and, as the truck started to move forward, I gave Champ an undetected, low whistle. Champ was athletic enough to jump into the back of the truck as my father was pulling away.

When we got to Moe's Food Fair Market, my father was upset and told me he had said he did not want the dog to come. I said, "He jumped in and I could not stop him." My father said, "He better not come into the store." I scolded Champ and told him to stay in the truck. As we were walking through the store aisles, we heard some commotion from the butcher area. Champ had made his way into the store and helped himself to a hefty serving of ground beef from behind the glass counter. The butcher chased Champ with a broom and yelled, "Whose dog is this?" Champ had red ground beef all over his snout and ran to my father for protection. The butcher asked my father, "Is this your dog?" Suddenly, my father could not speak English and said, "Yo no se íngles" (I don't know English). I quickly chased Champ from inside the store back to my father's truck. It was hilarious!

I just knew I was in big trouble based on the scowl my father had on his face. I was relieved when my father started laughing on the way home. He shook his head while saying, "What are we going to do with this dog?"

One time in a hard rainstorm, I flipped over in my bicycle loaded with newspapers as I hit the curbed sidewalk. Because of the running water, I could not see the driveway curb. I was really frustrated and not sure what to do next when my father drove up. I'm not sure how he found me as there were no cell phones nor GPS to track someone back then. My father helped me load my newspapers and bicycle onto his truck. That morning I finished delivering my route by hanging on to the side door and jumping on and off the side step of his truck. It was fun to get on and off the truck even while getting drenched because my father was there.

****

Many years later, my young son Ruben James was just learning how to ride his bicycle, and I coaxed him into riding his bike around our new house in the suburbs. I told him if he stayed on the sidewalk and just turned left four times, he would complete a circle and make it around the block. It was my way of getting him to explore his "hood" in Tempe.

I waited anxiously but he was taking too long, so I took a jog around the block and headed in the opposite direction. My son had gotten his pant leg tangled in the bicycle chain, and he toppled over with the bike on top of him. He was on the ground crying and could not get up as his pant leg was tangled in the bicycle chain. He was amazed that I was able to find him and stay with him to complete his ride back to our house. I told him I was proud of him for making it around the block and reassured him he would not need my help next time.

Note to Ruben: I will always remember your excitement before your fourth birthday. It was hard to get you to go to bed. The first thing you asked me in the morning was, "Is today, tomorrow?" I answered, "Yes!" Make the right choices TODAY so you will always enjoy tomorrow. You are a natural leader and I admire how you stand up for what you believe. I am proud of you and love you unconditionally. My prayer is that Casa Tamales is always filled with Love, Peace and Joy.

****

Even if you may no longer have your father or ever had father in your life, we always have our Heavenly Father watching over us. Nothing can separate us from the love God has for us, and He loves each of us the same. "Neither height nor depth, nor anything else in all creation, will be able to separate us from the love of God that is in Christ Jesus our Lord" (Romans 8:39).

Barrio lesson # 8 You have to hustle to make money.

CHAPTER 9

THE FIELD OF DREAMS

As a young boy, I loved the game of baseball. My favorite team was the San Francisco Giants, and I listened to many of their games on my small transistor radio that my father found at the dump. The Giants held their spring training in Phoenix and played games at the old Municipal Stadium on Central and Mohave. My father and Tio Mike took me to several games along with my cousins and brothers. We spent most of the game trying to retrieve foul balls.

After one of the games, my father put me on his shoulders and took me near the Giants' dugout. Somehow, among all the fanfare, the legendary Willie Mays reached up and shook hands with me. He was my favorite baseball player, and it thrilled me to shake hands with him. I just knew at that point that somehow through his touch, I would grow up to become a Major League Baseball player. Note: There is only One who had that kind of miraculous power. He used His special touch to make the blind see and lepers become as clean as a new eraser. When the woman with the issue of blood touched Jesus, He realized that power had gone out from him. Immediately her bleeding stopped. You can find this incredible story in Mark 5:24–33.

We used to spend endless hours in the empty lot in front of our house playing baseball in our makeshift field. My brothers and neighborhood friends even made baselines from flour we were able to sneak out of our houses. There was a house next to our field of dreams, and the young housewife would scream at us if we hit her house with a foul ball or an overthrow. There was one occasion when the ball ricocheted off her side door and it fell off the hinges. All of us kids scattered like cockroaches as she came out of her house screaming at us. Another elderly neighbor used to put on his baseball glove and sometimes managed to protect the windows of their laundry room from a home run. He was a good sport about the broken windows and would put a piece of plywood over it. He would say, "Lucy (his wife) complains that her laundry room gets too much sun." By the end of our baseball season, the laundry room was completely boarded up.

One day my friend Greedy showed up to play baseball wearing a brand-new set of glasses. He misjudged a pop-up and the ball hit him in the face and broke his glasses. He immediately started to cry, and I thought he was hurt. He said he was crying because he knew his mom would whip him with her glamour stretcher for breaking his new glasses. I remember getting hit by that no-good glamour stretcher and it hurt. She hit us because we had inserted some steelies (ball bearings we used to play marbles with) inside his younger brother's nose and we could not get them out. His younger brother went home screaming that he could not breathe. After Greedy's mom could not dislodge the steelies, she took him to the emergency room. She hit us several times with the glamour stretcher before leaving for the ER.

That darn glamour stretcher was a rubber stretch cord that was sold along with an exercise phonograph record and was demonstrated on television by Jack LaLanne in 1959. We used to make fun of Greedy's mom when we caught her doing her exercise routine done to the rhythm of organ music. In those days, adults other than your parents could also discipline you without any questions asked. Kids were kept in check back in the 1960s, at school, in restaurants, and at church. We were afraid of any adult and had to show them respect.

Phoenix summers were relentless, and my friends called me Toasty because my skin turned the color of toasted bread. I often joked later in life that my gang name was Toasty even though I did not join any hoodlum gangs.

I spent countless hours in the backyard pitching into the homemade BBQ structure my father and uncle put together. Mr. Meakin, our next-door neighbor, would sometimes give me pointers. He was probably in his sixties like I am now, and I thought he was ancient. He used to say, I am so old, I knew the Dead Sea when it was sick. I learned to hit the ball well and loved to pull the ball down the third baseline. Later in life this came in handy when I had more doubles than singles in the slow pitch USPS league.

There are many things that happened over the years, and it is difficult to pinpoint exact dates and the order in which things occurred.

As a family prior to my three youngest siblings being born, our family of six would go on rides on Saturday and sometimes to the drive-in movies. We frequented a hamburger joint near 19th Avenue and Maricopa regularly. The costs of hamburgers at Burger Queen were twelve for a dollar. Each of us, including my parents, would get to eat two apiece, and we shared a couple of large sodas. Life was simple then and special. My parents had their four oldest children every other year. There is a gap of seven years between Lupe and Lydia, who was born in July 1961. Ernie followed Lydia in December 1962 and Anita was born in January 1964. Papo was born in 1948, Richard in 1950, I in 1952, and Lupe in 1954. Real family is about a bond that cannot be broken by any means. Your family, related by blood or not, are the people who know you the best and still love you the most.

It was lots of fun to go to the drive-in and we really enjoyed seeing the cartoons in Technicolor. There was a playground in front of the big screen, and during the intermission, kid ran amuck on the teeter-totters and merry-go-round. The merry-go-round was pushed by hand, and you had to be careful getting on and off. I remember kids hanging on the iron apparatus and being dragged in circles until they finally let go. There was a trenched groove in the dirt surrounding the merry-go-round. This groove was created by kids circling the merry-go-round as they pushed it or were being dragged. In between the double features, the playground was invaded by an army of kids that created a cloud of dust.

Heading back to the car was challenging, and it helped us when dad flashed the headlights on his 1949 black Ford coupe. You had to be careful coming and going up and down on the raised rows for cars at the drive-in. Each spot had a speaker that was placed on the side of the window so you could hear the movie. There were times when the drive-in was not full, and we had to turn the volume up on nearby speakers so we could hear the movie better.

It was a special memory to see the newly released *Ben Hur* in November 1959. We took lots of snacks to the drive-in like tacos, popcorn, and big dill pickles. My father used to eat peas right from the can after he mixed some mayonnaise into them. At this point, my father was 35, mom was 32, Papo was 11, Richard was 9, I was 7, and Lupe was 5 years old. Going to the drive-in was always a special time for us. I wish there were still drive-ins now instead of drive-bys.

One of my fondest drive-in memories came when a message flashed across the screen prior to the first movie. It said to stay after the featured show to see the debut of Little Richard. My brother Richard said he was little Richard and we waited eagerly for the debut. When the young singer came on, he was outrageous as he sang "Good Golly, Miss Molly." He had wild hair, and his eyes seemed to dance while he played his piano. Little Richard helped define the era of rock 'n' roll with his flamboyant style using wails and screams. We laughed and called my brother Little Richard after that spectacular show.

My father loved his car and he hand painted it with a brush in a glossy black color. Unfortunately, we could scratch the enamel paint off it with our fingernails. Whenever he saw new scratches that were about kid height, he would examine our fingernails. My brothers and I were with him when he collided with a three-wheeled motorcycle near our house. Somehow the impact caused the driver and motorcycle to spin upright on one of the wheels like a top. We laughed out of control until my father sternly told us to be quiet. The young man was shaken but not hurt. He told my father it was his fault as he did not see our vehicle. We talked about the accident for several days and laughed every time we told someone about it.

As we got older, my parents would drop us (brothers and me) at the Fox Theater in Downtown Phoenix on Saturday afternoons. We used to go to Skaggs and could buy six candies for a quarter. We sometimes bought Sugar Daddies just to lick them and throw them off the balcony onto the seats below. Boy, I can only imagine now how ticked off I would be if I got hit on the back of the head by a slurped-on Sugar Daddy. Much of our time at the movies was spent running on the stairs. The attendants had no chance of catching us. They could have used an attendant named Elisha (more on this in the next chapter).

There were times when my parents did not show up to pick us up, so we had to walk home. The walk to our house was about two-and-a-half mile. We would walk on the railroad tracks and perfected our balance by walking on the rail. Sometimes we found metal strips used to seal transport boxes. We would cut the metal in a certain manner by bending it back and forth. Our goal was to get a small piece to form a vee and align the holes in the metal to make a whistling noise come out of it. Our railroad whistles had a rusty taste, but it took the sticky candy residue off our lips. We usually had our whistles confiscated at school the next day.

Around the age of sixteen or seventeen, I went to the Arizona State Fair with my sister Lupe. We got on a ride called the Flight to Mars that moved slowly through an enclosed area. There were props to make the short ride resemble Mars. When we got off the ride, Lupe told me a hairy hand had touched the back of her neck. I told her we were getting back on the ride so she could tell me when she felt the hairy hand. So, the moment we came in the ride and Lupe said, "Now!", I reached up and grabbed this person's hand and wrestled "the Martian" to the ground. After this I gave him a couple of playful but effective punches. It all happened so quickly that it caught this person completely off guard. I gave him a memory that was out of this world. Lupe began yelling for me to get back in the still-moving car before I got in trouble. I had to run to jump back into our spaceship. It was hilarious to show off for my sister and let her know a furry hand was not going to have its way with her. It doesn't matter if it is on Earth or Mars, I will always protect my sister(s) to the best of my ability.

There is no greater protection for us when we follow The Good Shepherd. In Jesus' words, "My sheep listen to my voice, I know them, and they follow me. I give them eternal life, and they shall never perish; no one will snatch them out of my hand, My Father, who has given them to me, is greater than all; no one can snatch them out of my Father's hand" (John 10:27–29).

Barrio lesson # 9 When you are being dragged by a merry-go-round, let go.

CHAPTER 10

THE RISE TO LEADERSHIP

During the fifth grade, there was a teacher who inspired me to learn, and it was the first time I received a straight A report card. Miss McDowell appointed me as the class president and told my classmates I was in charge if she had to step away from the classroom. Our classroom was a "cottage" that was detached from the main school building. One of my primary duties was to lock the cottage when we left and open the door after lunch and recess. It felt good to hold the small American flag as I led my classmates in reciting the Pledge of Allegiance as we began our school day. "Blessed is the Nation whose God is the Lord" (Psalm 33:12).

Some of the kids called me teacher's pet, but as the year went on, they did not mind me being in charge when Miss McDowell stepped away. There was a really cute girl named Cindy that had an interest in me. Even though she looked like Halle Berry, my agenda did not include girlfriends. During the summer prior to fifth grade, we (Sherman Street boys) formed a small club named the Monster club and our first rule was no girls allowed. We had weekly meetings and collected dues that we hid in a hole inside my dad's cuartito (small shack). We even designed our own club membership card as we pondered how we would help our country beat the Russians to the moon.

My fifth-grade teacher's birthday was on February 14 which is also

Arizona Statehood Day. On that special day, it is also Cupid's day to shoot arrows. As the class Prez, I was able to organize a surprise party where we brought in goodies and a small 45 rpm phonograph. With the help of the principal, he kept Miss McDowell away from the cottage long enough that afternoon for a surprise birthday celebration. She was touched to the point of tears and we had a blast. Before the party we rearranged our desks so we could have a limbo contest. "How low can you go?" For you youngsters, that's a lyric from that limbo song. We also had fun dancing to a new song by Chubby Checker called "The Twist." It was a moment that has stayed engrained in the walls of my memory bank, and when I hear that song, I always dance inside just like back then. What song makes you dance? Did you know King David knew how to dance? In Second Samuel 6 verse 14, it says, "David was dancing before the Lord with all his might, while he and all Israel were bringing up the ark of the Lord with shouts and the sound of trumpets." The story continues that his wife Michal (gift to David for defeating Goliath) saw King David leaping and dancing before the Lord and she despised him in her heart. I've often wondered if Michal felt upset because he was not acting like how she thought a king should behave. Maybe she was just plain jealous of the popularity King David had gained. Or, even worse, she was envious that she could not moonwalk like him.

My first formal baseball team was playing for Jackson Elementary School. Once I got over the fear of being hit by the pitch, I became a decent hitter. We had uniforms and had to get sponsors to purchase them. My sponsor was Al's Fish & Chips, so that's what it read on the back of my jersey. My teammates would yell, "Hey Al's Fish & Chips" when it was my turn to bat. Our coach, Mr. U, was a strict a strict disciplinarian who taught me how to focus and gain confidence. Our team went undefeated, and somewhere in the archives there is a picture of my team being the champions that year in an Arizona Republic clipping or in the microfilm of the Phoenix Library.

At the end of each game, we had to give the other team the obligatory "2-4-6-8, who do we appreciate" cheer as part of good sportsmanship.

We also had another cheer that Mr. U would not allow us to yell out. In the final championship game, I was blessed enough to get three hits in three at bats. My friend, Egghead (Edgar), referred to me as three for three after that game. We were ecstatic when we won the game, and we decided to give the losing school (Bethune) the other cheer. It went like this: "Chewdabacca! Chewdabacca! Spit on the wall! Bethune! Bethune! Can't play ball!" We piled into the back of Mr. U's pickup and told him to drive away quickly as rocks were being thrown at us. We continued our celebration yelling the forbidden cheer all the way back to Jackson school, we were the CHAMPS! I've learned now that it is better to stay humble after a victory. "Therefore, as it is written, 'Let the one who boasts, boast in the Lord'" (First Corinthians 1:31). Join me boasting by saying: All praise, glory, and honor to you Our Lord and Savior.

During that time there was a family of kids that liked to spend time at our house. My friend was nicknamed Shine-ola due to his dark skin color. They had moved to Arizona from Little Rock, and I enjoyed hearing their accent and the way they said things. For example, when they referred to something that belonged to them, they used the word, "we's" instead of "our." My brothers and I would devise ways to make them say we's by asking them something like, "Whose dog is that?" They would respond, "We's dog!" My father even joined in and called my friends, the We's dog family. I enjoyed spending time at their house because their father had perfected how to barbeque chicken. They were a solid Christian family and always prayed before every meal.

Shine-ola was an awesome friend and so were his younger twin brothers. I've always enjoyed paraphrasing MLK's quote that goes something like this: "I have a dream that one day a man will be judged by the content of their character and not the color of their skin." We still have a way to go as there is still discrimination against people of color and other differences.

I can't leave the fifth grade without mentioning my all-time favorite birthday in my entire life. It happened like this: after spending all day in the relentless desert sun playing baseball, my father told me and my baseball buddies to come over to the front porch. He made us banana splits with Neapolitan ice cream and used strawberry preserves for topping. I was impressed he was able to cut the entire length of the banana in half without breaking it. My father put a candle on my banana split and they sang "Happy Birthday" to me on my tenth birthday. For the record, to date, I have made it sixty-seven times around the sun. At this point, I want to give a shout out to my friends who taught me how to play baseball. The regulars were Ross the boss (RIP); Max (Lightbulb); the three Sample boys, Eugene (Gordo), Angel, and Rodney (Boots); Manuel (Greedy); Larry; and his younger brother Dennis. Thanks for the good times, and God bless all of you, along with my brothers and cousins, who were also out there in our sandlot.

Fifth grade and that period in my life were special and not complicated. I was excelling academically and felt good about contributing to the family finances. It bothered me to see my mother worried about how she was going to pay the monthly bills. In her frustration, she would take several household bills and throw them up into the air. When I asked her why she did this, she said the ones that landed face up would be paid that month. We were poor but always had enough; I never went without a meal.

About the only thing I can remember going wrong in the fifth grade happened like this. My buddy Mike and I were walking in the playground. From out of nowhere, someone threw a rock that struck Mike on the side of his cheek. The impact was so hard it knocked out one of his molars. Whoever threw that rock was fortunate that day that we did not have Elisha with us. Huh??? Elisha from the Old Testament had no tolerance for disrespectful kids.

"From there Elisha went up to Bethel. As he was walking along the road, some boys came out of town and jeered at him. "Get out of here baldy!" they said. "Get out of here baldy!" He turned around, looked at them and called down a curse on them in the name of the Lord. Then two bears came out of the woods and mauled forty-two of the boys" (2

Kings 2:23–24). Yes, this story is in the Bible. Elisha was more real than La Llorona or Freddy Krueger. Elisha had power from above.

Now that I was in the fifth grade, I had some good friends and friend-girls because most of us went to Our Lady of Fatima Catholic Church. We got to see the small church built from the ground up. Near the completion, my uncle and another parishioner got into a fist fight to determine who would have the privilege of painting the cross on top of the steeple. Neither one of them put the finishing touch as the priest double-crossed them (pardon the pun) by painting it himself.

One of the first things we were taught while being raised Catholic was: The One True, Holy, Catholic and Apostolic Church was the *only* church established by Jesus. We were taught this teaching came about after Jesus asked Peter, "who do you say I am." Peter told Jesus, "you are the Messiah, Son of the Living God." Jesus replied to Peter: "Blessed are you Simon, son of Jonah, for this was not revealed to you by flesh and blood, but by My Father in heaven. And I tell you that you are Peter, and on this rock I will build my church" (Matthew 16:16–18).

It is my opinion today the Catholic Church was not established after the above conversation between Jesus and Peter. However, I do believe on that day Christianity was built upon the rock. The rock refers to believing Jesus is the Son of God and He was sent to die for us as the Lamb of God. Having this type of faith in Jesus allows one to form a real personal relationship with Him and God the Father. There is no reference in the Bible to the Catholic Church being established by Jesus. If you are Catholic and reading this, please do not throw any rocks at me. This is my walk and where it has led me to believe like I do today. Being raised Catholic was a good starting point in my faith; reading the Bible completely several times has made it rock-solid.

Barrio lesson # 10 When you are put in charge, exceed what is expected of you.

CHAPTER 11

HOMERUN DISASTER

Jackson School was the home away from home for students in grades kindergarten through sixth grade. I had the privilege of going to school with many of the same students during these years. In November of that school year, our beloved President John F. Kennedy was assassinated. It was one of the saddest days in my life as school activities were brought to a halt so we could be told of the horrible news. I recall many of the teachers crying, and it seemed our country and world changed that day.

At home our family stayed glued to the black-and-white television for the next seven to ten days. After the suspect named Lee Harvey Oswald was caught, he was killed on national television by Jack Ruby while Oswald was under custody.

Not understanding all the conspiracy theories of the JFK assassination, as kids, we saw Jack Ruby as a hero because he killed the man that murdered our President. We would reenact the scene of Jack Ruby stepping out of a group of bystanders and shooting Oswald at point-blank range. The person who pretended to be Oswald had to make a distorted, full of pain look that comes from being shot in the stomach. There is still controversy as to who was behind the JFK killing to this day.

As a humorous sidenote, many years later, I was talking with three of my friends, one named Lee, one named Harvey, and the third one named

Oswald. A light went off in my head, and I abruptly stopped our conversation and pointed at each one of them with a puzzled look. I said, "Let's see, I have Lee, Harvey, and Oswald in front of me. I need to get out of here because there might be an assassination!" It was funny at the time, you had to be there.

The first homicide mentioned in the Bible is found in Genesis Chapter 4. It tells the story of Adam's two sons named Cain and Abel. In this short narrative, it describes how Cain's hatred fueled by jealousy toward his brother drove him to the point of murder. "Now Cain said to his brother Abel, 'let's go to the field.' While they were in the field Cain attacked his brother and killed him" (Genesis 4:8).

****

Have you ever been in such a rage in the heat of the moment that you could unintentionally kill someone? Perhaps it came from an argument after drinking too much, road rage, envy, or in a moment of protectiveness. My moment came in my early twenties at a wedding reception. I was part of the wedding party and looked dapper in my tuxedo. Things were going well, and then I experienced three levels of emotions. The first came when witnessing an argument that involved my oldest brother and his ex-wife. My brother screamed at me to grab her hands. She tried to scratch me, and it drew blood from her finger when she grabbed onto the straight pin that held my boutonniere. He and I had to carry his ex-wife out of the venue by her hands and feet. Fortunately, there were no i-Phones and YouTube back then. It was embarrassing as she was screaming and scratching all the way out. My mother was furious at her daughter-in-law for throwing a glass of beer on her. I had to assist my father and we had to force my beer-soaked mother into their car so my father could take her home. It was total chaos brought on by too much drinking which caused emotions to become out of control. After this second stage of emotions of being upset for having to physically pick up and place my mother into their vehicle, I thought the madness was over. I looked toward where my brother had parked his vehicle. I saw my brother being restrained by a man while my former sister-in-law's ex was landing punches on my brother's face. The third and worst emotion *rage* set into me for the first time in my life, and I saw the color of a blackish red as I ran to help my brother.

When I got there, I saw a stream of thick blood flowing down my brother's chin. I grabbed "the ex" from behind with my left arm around his neck in a choke hold and lifted him off his feet. In my out-of-control fury, I struck him several times in the forehead area and knocked him unconscious. The man holding my brother had to release him to stop me from continuing my assault. The incident happened in a matter of seconds, and everyone dispersed before the police got to the scene. I ended up with a broken bone in my hand and missed worked for several weeks. It could have been worse as it could have ended in involuntary manslaughter and incarceration. I'm thankful those before Christ (BC) days are long gone, and since I have learned to enjoy the fruit of the spirit. "But the fruit of the Spirit is love, peace, joy, patience, kindness, goodness, gentleness, faithfulness and self-control" (Galatians 5:22). I'm still working on self-control during the NFL season when the Dallas Cowboys lose.

****

The homerun disaster came toward the end of sixth grade. I had become a decent baseball player and was in top physical shape due to my bike riding associated with my morning and after-school paper routes. We had two sixth-grade classes at Jackson, and we competed against each other regularly in various sports during our last recess. Our rivalry was fierce and highly competitive as it gave bragging rights to the victor. Their class had some new kids that enrolled midway through the school year. These kids seemed to be more street savvy and rougher as they lived in the low-income housing near 15th Avenue and Buckeye. One of the kids named Beanie was thirteen years old (most sixth graders are eleven years old). I stayed away from Beanie as he was a loud and boisterous bully. He could have passed for Clubber Lang's son from the movie, *Rocky II*.

Anyway, the homerun disaster happened near the end of one of our sixth-grade competitive baseball games. It was one of the most unfair things that happened to me in life. I was a darn good kid with straight As. How many eleven-year olds do you know that could deliver newspapers before and after school seven days per week? During this baseball game, my class was trailing by a couple of runs, but we were batting in our final inning. It was the perfect scenario when it was my turn to bat. There were two runners on base, and I was able to hit the ball perfectly. The ball sailed way over the left fielder's head almost to the swings. My classmates were cheering as I rounded the bases and getting ready to score the winning run. Beanie was upset and stood in the way of me crossing home plate. There were no coaches or teachers monitoring our game. I tried to tell him we won fair and square. He was pissed at me and told me to shut up. Since there was no adult presence, he began punching me and gave me a good beating. It was shocking and unfair to go from a hero to getting pummeled by a bully and losing all dignity in a blink of an eye. I wish I could see Beanie today so I could challenge him and beat the crap out of him now. (Note to reader: This part was written about two years ago, and since then, I have forgiven him… more on forgiveness to follow.)

My feelings were really hurt because none of my friends, some of who I had defended before, tried to intervene to stop Beanie. I went home sobbing without going back to the classroom after recess. My pants were torn and I had blood on my knee, and my head throbbed with every step I took. My nose had a trickle of blood that I smeared onto my forearm. I also felt a "small mouse" forming under my left eye. When I got home, my Tia Tillie was visiting my mom. They were both surprised to see me crying and home from school about an hour ahead of schedule. My aunt was livid when I told them what had happened; she used some strong and colorful language I did not expect from her. My mother just said, "You better toughen up, boy!" My aunt went on to say, "We are getting in my car right now so we can go find this 'pendejo' (means more than stupid).

I'm going to hold him down and you are going to beat the (expletive) out of him!" I was worried and told my aunt he was pretty tough. She looked at me with a scowl that would have made Jack Nicholson jealous and said very emphatically "He doesn't know what tough is!!!"

Next thing I knew we were in her car and on a mission to seek and destroy. We went looking for him on what I thought would be his route home to his roach-infested, ghetto tenement (I was upset when I wrote this the first time). We did not find him that day and it was probably better for two reasons:

1. My Tia Tillie could not be with me every day for the remainder of sixth grade.
2. It was 1964 and I did not learn the crane kick from *The Karate Kid* movie until 1984 (LOL).

After the homerun disaster, I feared meeting up with Beanie while I was on my paper route after school. My worry was he would take away any money my customers had paid me for paper delivery. My confidence was shaken, and I used to practice making mean faces in front of the mirror. Beanie never bothered me again and I'm so thankful God is in control. Perhaps, God gave me an advance on protection even though at the time, I did not have a personal relationship with him. After all, it does say in the Book of Proverbs 16:7, "When the Lord takes pleasure in anyone's way, He causes their enemies to be at peace with them." My comfort now comes from knowing this promise, "The Lord himself goes before you and will be with you; he will never leave you nor forsake you. Do not be afraid; do not be discouraged" (Deuteronomy 31:81).

Post note: The night I wrote this chapter, I reread it and the realization came to me that I still had bitterness over this incident. I prayed and asked God to shine His light into my heart and remove my unforgiveness toward Beanie. God took care of it, and in this forgiving process, it removed this defect and healed my heart. The remarkable thing about forgiving someone even though it might be the last thing you want to do—it sets the prisoner free. The prisoner is not the person who did you wrong, the prisoner is really you. Sometimes the offender has no clue you are holding a grudge. The poison from the unforgiveness hardens your heart and takes away life flow with thoughts of revenge or other forms of wishing evil on your offender.

Whoever that person is, make time to forgive them and move on with life more freely. It is good for your heart, almost like eating Applejacks, the slogan used to be "a bowl a day keeps the bullies away."

On the serious note, I end this chapter which was difficult to write with: "For if you forgive other people when they sin against you, your Heavenly Father will also forgive give you" (Matthew 6:14). It would be eternally catastrophic to be denied Heaven due to unresolved issues with someone who offended you. Even if you don't speak to the offender, have a conversation with God, and ask Him to remove the venom from your thoughts and heart.

Barrio lesson # 11 Bullies can ruin your homerun trot.

CHAPTER 12

PICKLE-COLORED EYES

Growing up we spent a lot of time with my cousins. My Tia Tillie (RIP) was my mother's sister and my Tio Joe (RIP) was my dad's first cousin. This would make my siblings and me more than first cousins to their offspring. We saw them regularly at our house, at their house, and at church. My cousins were five brothers and one sister, while we were three brothers and one sister. It made an instant army of kids at our get-togethers. All of us ten kids were born between 1948 and 1955. I guess my parents and tios took it literally when they read the instruction from God to be fruitful and increase in number.

My sister and my girl cousin Bestest were the youngest. Bestest has always been like a sister to me, and she used to love honey. She only shared her honey with my sister and me, her bestest.

My mother and Tia were strict disciplinarians that managed to keep us eight rowdy young boys in check with just "that look." We had no video games or fancy toys, but we would play football, wrestling, race, hide-and-seek, kickball, dodgeball, red rover, and any other game to the point of exhaustion. My tios would later have five more boys and one more baby girl cousin named Lizzie. My cousin Danny and I were the youngest of the first set of boys. Our nickname was "the bears" due to our wrestling each other like cubs. I give lots of credit to my parents and tios for feeding all those hungry mouths. There were times my mother and tia would be in the kitchen cooking up a storm while we sat at the table and chanted, "We want food! We want food! We want food, right now, Today!"

At this point, I need to interject a special memory of my mom and tia dancing "La Bamba" when the young Richie Valens first released this song in 1958. My mom and tia practiced their dance moves while swatting away eight young boys who tried to join in their dance. This was completely out of character to see them in their peddle pusher pants and watch their beauty and grace while they perfected their dance. It was a special blessing to see them enjoying themselves instead of being mom and having to keep us in line. My mother and tia were such a blessing to us, and I want to honor them with the words found in Proverbs 31: 27–29, "She watches over the affairs of her household and does not eat the bread of idleness. Her children arise and call her blessed; her husband also, and he praises her: 'Many women do noble things, but YOU surpass them all.'"

My Tia Tillie has always been special to me and has given me "sugar" aka kisses all my life for as long as I could remember. She would chuckle as she asked my brother Richard for brown sugar as he was more prieto (darker skinned) than me. My Tia Tillie was the one who blessed me prior to leaving Arizona in 1990. I praise God she was so instrumental in my life and is now rejoicing in Heaven and I get to see her again. I am confident my parents and tios are there in Heaven perhaps watching a rerun of *The Beverly Hillbillies* or Roller Derby. There were many evenings we spent watching television after we adjusted the "rabbit-ear" antennas that had to sit perfectly on the TV to get a clear picture. Sometimes the television would go off and there would be wording on the screen that read, PLEASE STAND BY. Cousin Danny would run and stand next to the television. He was always quick to take action just like a firefighter.

Now that my parents and most of my tios have passed, here are my thoughts on death. I believe when we die, it is like the feeling you get when waking up from anesthesia. One moment you're asleep and in an instant you are awake. I base this belief from Colossians 2:5 "For though I am absent from you in body, I am present with you in spirit." Here is more on thoughts about death: they that love us beyond this world cannot be separated from us by death. There are constant reminders of them like the smell of their perfume or cologne; someone that looks like them; remembering a special saying; their favorite meal, song, or restaurant; a television show; or a memory no one, not even death, can take from you. Death cannot kill what never dies.... They are in heaven waiting for us.

Here's part of a poem I wrote called "Just for us" shortly before my mother's passing into heaven:

Giving us life inside of her womb,

Teaching her children, the right way to groom.

Loving us always all of her life,

Now living in her eternal reward.

Planned by the Father

Just forever, just for us.

Death is not final. "Where, O death, is your victory? Where O death, is your sting?" 1 Corinthians 15:55 You don't scare me—I am a child of the Living God.

When my cousins left our house after spending the day with us, we would yell out, "bye!" as my tio drove away. They would yell back, "bye!" and this would go on for five or six goodbye exchanges before we could no longer hear them. These are special memories of cousins, primo hermanos (brother/sister cousins), who went on to be some of the finest firemen and police officers to serve the City of Phoenix, along with several of their children. At this point, I want to thank all my cousins for always embracing my brother Ernie, especially Alfie. My cousin Al has made it a point for years to have a five-dollar bill sticking out of his back pocket when Ernie is around. As Ernie hugs him, he manages to snag the five spot. It is hilarious to watch as Al pretends to not know what is happening while Ernie runs off with his gift.

My parents did their best to "keep up with the Jones" (my tios) and this benefitted us. When they bought a new car, we got a new car. If they took a vacation, we took a vacation. I remember feeling jealousy for the first time around the age of five. This happened when my cousins went to the recently opened Disneyland. It was difficult to listen to their awesome trip; I must have heard how little Danny got lost on Main Street about seven times. If my jealousy could have spoken, it would have screamed, "Who cares! You obviously found him because he's here in front of me wearing his Mickey Mouse hat!" At that point my eyes must have turned green like a pickle as I was feeling super "jelly." That's a term young people use today instead of saying jealous. In keeping up with those Jones, guess what? We got to go to Disneyland near the end of 1958. I must remember to rejoice at others' good news; my time will come when I get old enough.

Here are a couple of memories from our visit to Disneyland. The first is when we got to ride on the locomotive that circled the park. During this train ride, some cowboys entered our compartment and began shooting their six guns as part of a fake train robbery. My sister Lupe screamed, "Aye mamacita, me matan, me matan!" (Mommy, mommy, they are going to kill me). The people on the train erupted in laughter.

The second memory occurred when we were riding in an open-air tram en route to our car in one of the huge parking lots. My parents had bought us plastic yellow hats that had a long bill to resemble Donald Duck. As the tram picked up speed, my sister's hat flew off. My father, who was sitting a few spaces from her, was quick enough to catch her hat in mid-air. My sister went from heartbreak to pure joy in three seconds flat. It would have made a great America's Funniest Video. It felt special to tell my friends and cousins that we had gone to Disneyland. Here are a couple of things that went wrong when Disneyland opened on July 17, 1955.

- On opening day, workers were still planting trees and some areas still had wet paint.
- There were counterfeit tickets, and over twice the number of guests showed up to attend opening day festivities.
- Each park ticket had a designated time to enter and leave, but the guests who got there early were not leaving at their designated time.
- Due to increased visitors from counterfeit tickets, the Disneyland restaurants and refreshment stands ran out of food and beverages.
- The asphalt on Main Street was still wet from the prior night's rain, and women's high heels were sticking in the pavement.

Disneyland opening day was referred to as Black Sunday by the cast members. The following verse is so true in this case: "In their hearts humans plan their course, but the Lord establishes their step" (Proverbs 16:9).

Getting back to the subject of jealousy, I still haven't gotten over the time my cousins went with my tios to Flagstaff. When they returned to Phoenix, there was still actual snow on top of their car. I tried to touch the snow, but my older cousin Joey pushed my hand away because "It will melt." They went on to describe how they built a snowman and rode inner tubes in the snow. Once again, my eyes turned the color of a pickle. We did not make it to the snow as a family because my mother did not like cold weather, and when momma ain't happy... we weren't going nowhere!"

Barrio lesson #12 Rejoice at others' good news...my time will come when I am old enough

CHAPTER 13

THE EMBARRASSMENT TIMES THREE

It was a Sunday afternoon and my uncle (RIP) came to visit us. On this day he really gave me one of my most embarrassing moments in my life. This happened when we went to the neighborhood convenience store named Sargent's Market. It was in the early 1960s before the plethora of 7-Elevens and Circle Ks.

He was my dad's older brother and loved to tell stories. The best way to describe him is at that time he looked like the Hispanic version of the Fonz mixed with Wayne Newton. He always told us (my two brothers and three cousins) if we were not good boys, the tecolotito would get us. I never knew exactly what the tecolotito was (small owl), but it sounded scary enough to keep me in line. He was good at storytelling, and his eyes would always get wide like he was "asusustado" (scared). I would pay to have a recorded video of him so I could still hear him say, "Ay vengo por mi pata de oro!" (I'm coming for my foot made of gold) one more time. This was a ghost story about a pirate that had his peg leg made of gold stolen from him. He also told an excellent story of La Llorona, and when he told the story, he would suddenly look behind us as if he had just seen her. It scared the dickens out of us, and we had to sleep with the light on.

My uncle was a different kind of person when he drank too much. Sometimes my aunt would have to wear dark sunglasses at night. Unfortunately, I witnessed him being rough with my cousins during a family spat when they tried to protect their mom. My uncle worked at the Phoenix brick house near 7th Avenue and the Black Canyon Freeway. He used to come home bright red like a lobster from working all day in the heat and being close to the brick ovens. I felt sorry for him because where he worked was hotter than a jalapeño in a microwave.

My mother told me that my uncle and father were once approached by female tourists at a park near Hole-in-the-Rock because they thought they were Native Americans. They took several photos, and my uncle enjoyed having his arms around the tourists as they posed for the pictures. His face was always red from working near the brick ovens, and he made up his own Indian sign language to keep us entertained. He was sometimes like a walking Pictionary game and we had to guess what he was trying to tell us.

There was another time when he took us to get some pecans. He was fearless as he climbed high up on a pecan tree and shook it as hard as he could to make the ripe pecans fall from the tree. As he shook the tree, he would yell, "Charracate! Charracate!" I'm not sure what that word meant; maybe it was passed down from our Aztec ancestors. The word "Charracate" seemed to give him the strength of a large orange chango (orangutan). Words can help you gain more power. I never used the word Charracate, but when I must muster extra strength or focus, I use the verse found in Philippians 4:13: "I can do all things through Christ who strengthens me."

Unlimited pecans hit us as we stood underneath as my uncle shook the tree. He told us, "Hurry up! We gotta go before anyone notices we are here!" When we left, we had more pecans than you could shake a tree at. In Proverbs 9:17, it reads, "Stolen water is sweet; food eaten in secret is delicious!" The pecan pies my mother and aunt made for us later that week sure were sweet and delicious!

Getting back to the first embarrassment, my father and uncle were having a couple of cold Coors one Saturday afternoon when they discovered we had no toilet paper in the house. My uncle had the urge to splurge (go to the bathroom) in a bad way. My uncle invited my brothers, three male cousins, and me to go to the neighborhood store with him. We quickly walked through the barrio and went to Sargent's Market about 4 short blocks away. We had fun watching my uncle do an exaggerated poop walk. He walked like he had cramps running up and down both of his hamstrings, and he looked like he was carrying his posterior.

Inside the store, I saw a couple of my friends including my beloved "Lala." As my uncle approached the cash register with one measly roll of toilet paper, Sarge remarked, "You are only buying one roll of toilet paper with all these six boys?" My uncle always had a quick response and said, "You see Sir, it's like this (there was a pause and he pointed at the six of us)....These boys don't wipe their behind!" He used a stronger word other than behind. In those days, we did not curse, and my virgin ears were stunned to hear the A-word. The small store erupted in laughter like a Fluffy comedy show. I must have blushed about ten shades of red. We tried to yell out, "Yes we do!", but it was too late as our pleas were not heard over the laughter. After that incident, I was never able to look at Sarge straight in the eyes again.

After finishing sixth grade, most Jackson School kids went to Grace Court to finish their seventh and eighth grade. My parents decided that my sister Lupe and I would go to St. Matthews located on 21st Avenue and Van Buren the following school year. My getting pummeled by Beanie probably helped make the decision for us to go to Catholic school. This was a burden on the family financially as my parents now had to pay tuition. My two younger sisters had the benefit of going to St. Matthews from first to eighth grade. My youngest sister Anita likes to say she is not afraid of anything because she was taught by nuns.

At my new school, it was weird to be the new boy at a small, private Catholic school. Their curriculum was more advanced than what I had learned during my studies at Jackson school. I had to pick up how to multiply with decimals and somewhere missed a step or two. One of the benefits of going to St. Matthews was I reconnected with Lala who only went to Jackson for kindergarten. It was like Visine for my eyes to see Lala changed so much from the last time I had seen her. She had transformed into a stunning young lady even in her Catholic school uniform. She had green eyes that sparkled, and her light brown hair had natural streaks of vibrant colors. She usually had a smile on her face that could melt a snowman. At one point during our "grown-up" friendship, Lala asked me, "What would you do if I kissed you?" I was stunned by her question and could not react. (snooze, you lose) I shrugged my shoulders, so nothing ever happened.

My second most embarrassing moment in academia came during a spelling session. My seventh-grade teacher was a nun named Sister Mary Dominic. Our nickname for her was Sister Mary Dynamite due to her fiery and explosive temper. Sister Mary Dynamite as we called her asked me to spell the word "choose." Growing up learning Spanish before English made it difficult for me to distinguish the sound or say words beginning with sh and ch. For example, for chicken and cheese, I would say shicken and sheese. Anyway, when the Nun asked me to spell "choose," I asked her, "Is it what you wear on your feet or when you have to pick something." The class roared with laughter; the Nun let me off the hook by asking me to spell the word "Mississippi."

Did you know that Moses had a problem with stuttering? God had told Moses to tell the Pharaoh to set Israelites free. This story is at the end of Exodus Chapter 6. After Moses received his instruction from God, he responded, in Exodus 6:30, "But Moses said to the Lord, 'Since I speak with faltering lips, why would the Pharaoh listen to me?'" It was a simple fix for God, He told Moses his brother Aaron would speak for him.

My third humiliation came during my senior year in high school. Being a lifelong Phoenix Suns fan since 1968, I went on my very first date to attend one of their games. As I arrived at the Suns basketball game, my date (no it was not Lala) and I were looking for our seats way up in the nosebleed section in a sold-out arena. It was awkward trying to squeeze in between people while carrying popcorn and two sodas. From seats about seven rows higher than mine, I heard someone yelling, "Hey Pailhead!" I ignored the yelling a couple of times as I was too cool to look up to see who was making all the ruckus. Then I heard, "YOU! Pailhead! Look up here!" When I glanced up, I made eye contact with my father's cousin Louie. He was waving at me frantically and pointed at me while laughing and shouted, "Enjoy the game, Pailhead!" The entire section 316 joined in his laughter. My date asked me why is that man calling me pailhead. I told her I would explain later as the game was about to begin. It was a memorable mortification, and to this day, almost fifty years later, we still call each other pailhead. It is all in fun…. Laughter is medicine to the soul.

Note: Maybe, God will bless me with my Simeon moment, and I'll get to see the Suns win an NBA championship before I die (LOL). Let me explain through this scripture, "Now there was a man in Jerusalem called Simeon, who was righteous and devout. He was waiting for the consolation of Israel, and the Holy Spirit was on him. It had been revealed to him by the Holy Spirit that he would not die before he had seen the Lord's Messiah" (Luke 24, 25–26). The story goes on and about when Joseph and Mary presented Jesus at the temple courts; Simeon took baby Jesus in his arms and praised God because he knew he could now die in peace. I can only imagine what it will be like to experience being with our Savior, forget this reference to the Suns winning a championship, I'm fixing my eyes on the real Prize, that is, getting to hear the words, "Well done!" when I enter through the pearly gates and walk on the Street (singular) of gold. Here's something to look at when you read in the Book of Revelation. When there is reference to streets in Heaven, it is mentioned in the singular (street) form. Another interesting tidbit is found in Revelation 21:21. "The twelve gates were twelve pearls, each gate made of a single pearl. The great street of the city was of gold, as pure as transparent glass." Now use your imagination to think about the size of an oyster that could produce a gate-sized pearl. Like Lisa Pisa would say, "Fascinating!"

Barrio Lesson #13: Never go to the store with your uncle that is tipsy.

CHAPTER 14

ALTAR BOYS

There were many hours spent at catechism between my age of seven and thirteen years old at Our Lady of Fatima Catholic Church. Our teachings were held inside the small church, and we were told to stay quiet because Jesus lived inside the small box on the altar. Early on I would try to figure out how Jesus lived inside the small tabernacle. The other thing that turned my brain into menudo was thinking too long about God having no beginning and no end. During those years I learned how to pray two main prayers as a youth, the Our Father and the Hail Mary. We also prayed numerous rosaries during those formative years. There is so much more freedom and meaning for me now when talking to God through prayer that comes directly from my heart.

When Jesus taught his disciples how to pray, he prefaced the Our Father prayer by saying, "And when you pray, do not keep on babbling like pagans, for they think they will be heard because of their many words. Do not be like them, for your Father knows what you need before you ask him" (Matthew 6: 7–8).

I had the honor of being an altar boy shortly after making my First Communion. The masses back then were said in Latin, so we had to memorize responses to what the priest said during the service. There was a long prayer called the Confiteor that is a lengthy confession prayer in

Latin said near the beginning of mass. Since we did not know the prayer and had difficulty memorizing Latin, we mumbled some noise. During this part, an altar boy kneeled and had to bend while kneeling with his head down low. While we were low and our head was almost to the floor, we pretended to be praying in Latin. Prior to coming up from being bent low, we beat our breast three times while saying, "Mea culpa! Mea culpa! Mea maxima culpa!" because that's how the prayer and ritual ended. Mea culpa is equivalent to how young kids today say "my bad" when they make a mistake.

Prior to the mass, we had to get the water and wine ready for the upcoming service. Sometimes we managed to sneak in a little taste before the priest arrived. During one of the masses, the other altar boy serving with me tripped and kicked the handheld bells that were used during the service; it was spectacular. The clattering filled the whole church and my altar partner was super embarrassed. The bells seemed to tumble in slow motion as Ricky tried to catch up with them while stumbling. I barely kept from laughing that day, and the sound of the bells echoed through my head for the entire mass. I playfully told Ricky afterward he was going to get arrested for underage drinking.

There was another occasion when Ricky had an epileptic seizure while serving with Max and me. We did not know what to do. Good thing Mr. U was there because he hurdled the communion rail and carried Ricky to the pews while he recovered. As kids, we were told that a person having a seizure like this could swallow their tongue, so it gave us a minor scare.

When people came up and kneeled to receive communion, we held a golden plate attached with a handle to place under the person's chin as they received the host from the priest. When certain friends came up, I would sometimes give them a little tap on throat as their mouth was wide open while having their eyes closed. It was one of those games of composure to see who could be the most travesio (mischievous) without laughing or getting caught. I guess we wouldn't have made it entering the Holy of Holies back in the Old Testament. When God gave the responsibility to the Levites to do the work associated with the priesthood, it came in part with the following instructions: "But only you and your sons may serve as priests in connection with everything at the altar and inside the curtain. I am giving you the service of priesthood as a gift. Anyone else who comes near the sanctuary is to be put to death" (Number 18:7).

During the summer, I would serve mass at 6 am prior to becoming a paperboy. One hot summer late afternoon, after playing baseball most of the day, I fell asleep under the evaporative cooler. When I woke up, I looked at the clock and saw it was almost 6. I scrambled to my feet and gruffly said to my mom, "You should have woke me up!" as I rushed past her in the kitchen. She chuckled and did not say a word. I hurried out of our back gate and started trotting toward the church. Going down our alley, I passed the old lady's house that we liked to harass. I looked at the sky and wondered why the sun was behind me. Then it hit me… Tonto campana! (Dumb bell!)—it was 6 pm instead of 6 am. When I made it back to the house, my mother was laughing and then gave me a big hug. She told me she was proud of me for being so anxious to help the priest.

I hope you caught the part about going past the old lady's house that we liked to harass. There was an old lady (Julia's mom) that lived in a small shack that had an aluminum roof. The shack was detached from Julia's house and sat at the edge of the alley with no fence. My brothers and I would send high rock trajectories that crashed loudly on her tin roof from our backyard. We could hear her scream, "Hay demonios!" (There's demons), but we would stay quiet so we would not get caught. There were other boys in our neighborhood and our thinking was they would be blamed.

We used to go by her house and bang on her wooden walls to get an instant, loud reaction. We made our best ghost noises and my brother Papo would yell, "Soy el diablo!" (I'm the devil). One evening my mom sent us to the store, and of course, on our way, we pounded on the old lady's wall. When we got home, my mom was on the phone with Julia. She looked disgusted and I knew we were busted. They had solved the mystery of our harassment, and as punishment, we had to cut their grass for the remainder of that summer. We also had to apologize to the old lady in Spanish. It was super embarrassing to face Julia after that incident. Julia sold burritos from her house and they were delicious. I would not have blamed her if she added a little spit in our food after we had been so disrespectful toward her mother. In the Book of Leviticus 19:32, it reads: "Stand up in the presence of the aged, show respect for the elderly and revere your God, I am the Lord." I sincerely regret doing this as a young boy, and I knew back then that it was wrong but could not help doing it anyway. There are times when you say or do something wrong, but once it happens, like my tata (grandfather) would say, "you can't unring the bell!"

The apostle Paul wrote about wanting to do right but couldn't and being unable to stop doing wrong. "For I do not do the good I want to do, but the evil I do not want to do – this I keep on doing" (Romans 7:19).

We got into serious trouble on a packed-out Good Friday service in the spring of 1966. My BFF Jimmy Vaughn and I were altar boys at St. Matthew's and served during the stations of the cross. He carried a large crucifix on a pole, while I carried a tall lit candle. At the conclusion of the stations, the priest would say "Blessed be God" and the congregation would repeat "Blessed be God." There were several repetitions of what the priest said. Prior to the service when we were putting on our altar boy attire, Jimmy told me when he says, "Blessed be the Holy Spirit, the Paraclete," I'm going to repeat, "Blessed be the Holy Spirit, the parakeet." I begged him not to say it. The service was solemn with incense burning and people feeling emotional over what happened to Jesus on Good Friday. True to his word, Jimmy Vaughn repeated, "Blessed be the Holy Spirit, the *parakeet!*" We immediately both lost it and started laughing; I heard a couple of parishioners chuckle. Father Murphy turned bright red and stopped while we laughed. We felt foolish and finally gained our composure enough to be able to finish the service. Later in the changing room, Father Murphy scolded us profusely like a boss. We had to kneel for an hour on the concrete for our punishment.

****

You can make atonement for things you wish you would not have done in your youth especially when you learn what good behavior is. After accepting Jesus as my Lord and Savior, I was blessed to receive one-on-one teaching from an excellent teacher. After several weeks under her tutelage, she asked me, "Ruben, que es bueno?" (What is good?) I wanted to impress her, so I gave her a long list of doing and being good. She kept asking me, "Es todo?" (Is that all). I racked my brain and covered everything from Loving God with all my heart and soul to stopping to help elderly cross the street. My list was lengthy and would have made Santa Claus bankrupt if I followed it. She then looked at me with a twinkle in her eye and smiled so I thought I had passed the test. She followed with, "Open your bible to the Book of James Chapter 4 and read verse 17." I hurried and much to my astonishment, it reads, "If anyone knows the good they ought to do and doesn't do it, it is sin for them." Wow! What a life lesson I received that Sunday morning in January 2000 at Primera Baptist Church. Thank you, Hermana Diana!

Barrio lesson #14 You can't un-ring the bell

CHAPTER 15

TIME'S FUN WHEN YOU'RE HAVING FLIES

My best friend in eighth grade at St. Matthew's was named Jimmy Vaughn. He was 6'6" and only 14 years old. Many people were intimidated by him including my two older brothers. We were right on the verge of getting into trouble as we explored the barrio while flexing our young muscles. Jimmy used to peer over the top of privacy doors in the occupied stalls at the bus station bathroom. He would say in his deepest voice, "Hey! What are you doing down there?" He would then spit on their head as they sat on the pot. We would then turn off the lights and run out of there. No one ever pursued us, but it sure felt like someone was coming after us.

One day we found a new means to entertain ourselves after school. Behind the Arizona State Capitol, there were some large exhaust fans that worked in conjunction with the air conditioner. We discovered that if we spit into the grate while the air was blowing, it would take our spit into the air and sometimes suspend it for a few seconds. We spent over an hour spitting into the grate and enjoyed watching our spit float upward. We *laughed* until our faces hurt. This chapter will cover "a time to weep and a time to laugh, a time to mourn and a time to dance" (Ecclesiastes 3:4).

We spent lots of time at each other's house, and Jimmy's mother used to call me Ruben the rabbit. She called me this because she said I ran like a rabbit while carrying the football and when I zigzagged, no one could catch me. She *laughed* when she told me this and made buckteeth while putting her index fingers above her ears like she was a rabbit. Jimmy and I would also *laugh* when I batted against his pitching at baseball practice. He could throw a wicked curve ball that would break for a strike after it looked like the pitch was about to hit you. Sometimes he would *laugh* and tell me, "This one is not going to curve and it's going to hit you in the &%$#" (family jewels). I would tell him, "If it doesn't curve, I will hit the ball right back at you and hit you where it will make your voice change, again." It was still our *time to laugh*.

My other friends in eighth grade included Joe and Gabe, who had both decided to go into the seminary in California. Joe had two sisters that were fun to hang around with, and they teased us because we went to a Catholic school. I remember going to Joe's house to watch a baseball game for my first time on a newly purchased color television.

During those days, we went to Catholic Youth Organization *dances* at Our Lady of Fatima. It was our *time to dance*. Those were the wonder years, and when I learned to dance the Jerk and the Louie Louie at the small church hall. In those early 1960s, James Brown was a phenomenal showman and could do the splits while *dancing* better than anyone (my cousin Pete could do them pretty good). While James Brown was on stage, he would pretend to break down emotionally and had to take a break. Members of his band called The Flames would console him by placing his cape on him. This would revive him, and he jumped back onto the stage and danced like he was the Father of Soul; it was spectacular.

Those days were special as we would go on youth outings in the church bus. Some of the older girls would lead the busload of youth in songs like "Downtown" by Petula Clark. Three of these young ladies also entertained us by imitating The Supremes and singing "Stop in the Name of Love."

Part of our eighth-grade curriculum included putting on a Broadway-type show for the seventh-grade class. Our production used several scenes from the popular movie, *Mary Poppins*. Several of us boys had to do a quick step to a song from the movie called *Step in Time*. We had fun linking our elbows while we stepped in time. The young lady (Lala's best friend) who was kind of my girlfriend did a great job at singing, "Loverly." This was our show and our *time to dance*.

During this school year, my kind of a girlfriend (back then I didn't know how to have full-fledged girlfriend) invited me to see the newly released movie, *The Sound of Music*. This young lady and her mother picked me up in their family car, since we were too young to drive. We had a fabulous time at the movies, and it made my heart skip a beat to catch this nice-looking young lady glancing over at me. When I got home, my mother told me she thought the girl was too forward by inviting me to a movie. She also referred to my friend's mother as *vieja alcahueta*. I did not know what that meant at the time, so I looked it up; it roughly translates to woman pimp. My mother's eyes turned the color of a pickle. She did not approve of anyone I dated until she met Irma.

Around that time, we (my brothers and I) had outgrown the paper routes and would find daywork on Saturdays in the onion fields near Peoria. My brother Papo could now drive and had a 1956 Chevrolet that was nicknamed the bumblebee. Guess what color it was? Getting to the onions was a chore as it seemed so far away. When we got there, the work was way more difficult than delivering newspapers. It seemed like the onion fields stretched all the way to the edge of the earth. The fresh-cut onions would burn our eyes and I felt like I was about to *weep*. It was surreal as no one talked, and if they did, the Filipino slave driver was there instantly to stop the conversation. This boss must have been a descendant of Nebuchadnezzar as we stayed kneeled before him all day (Daniel Chapter 3). We got paid $1.25 an hour and after eight hours returned home with an onion-scented ten-dollar bill. I'll never forget the sting from getting onion juice on the nicks on my hands caused by the erratic shears I used to snip the tops off countless onions.

When we got home, my father would always tell us, "One day of field-work does not compare to what I had to do as a child." He said he only attended school until third grade because he had to work all day from sunrise to sunset to bring home money for the family. I asked him if they got breaks and he said only to eat one time during the day. When I asked him how they determined the time to eat (wristwatches were not common back in the 1930s), he said they would put a stick in the ground and when there was no shadow (high noon), it was time to eat. He said he worked picking cotton and boxing strawberries, peaches, lettuce, and tomatoes. One of my jokes back then was to tell my friends that my father was a professional boxer. He was undefeated as he boxed lettuce, tomatoes, and strawberries.

My father knew a farmer in Queen Creek (my first Postmaster office many years later) that would let us go glean his fields after the harvest was made. We took a truckload of potatoes home and then sold potatoes around our neighborhood for twenty-five cents per bucket. Our neighbor, George, was so pleased with the price that he bought two buckets for his family (his mom, his wife Carol, and their two daughters, Sandy and Shelly). When we sold all the potatoes that were edible, then we divided the remaining potatoes among our neighborhood friends. We formed two teams, and we had a rotten potato fight. By the time the battle was over, we smelled worse than dead skunks with bad breath. I remember using trash can lids for protection against those flying spuds. Today, for protection, I put on the armor of God found in Ephesians Chapter 6 verses 13–17 "Therefore put on the full amour of God, so that when the day of evil comes, you may be able to stand your ground, and after you have done everything, stand firm." At this point I ask the reader to look up what battle pieces come with the Armor of God. These pieces of armor can be found in Ephesians 6 verses 14–17. You'll read how this armor prepares you for spiritual battle.

Our family at home was complete, and my three youngest siblings were just toddlers. Anita (Baby Jumbo) was the youngest and only thirteen months younger than Ernie (Stinky Beak). Lydia (China Doll) was already their babysitter and trying to make tortillas. Ernie and Anita got into some serious baby fights; they did not like each other. She would bite him, and he would stagger her with a well-placed headbutt. We were a poor but happy family. Things got easier when the house was expanded with a dining room, another bedroom with a shower.

It was a St. Matthew's tradition for the seventh graders to send off the eighth graders by reading individual proclamations of predicting an eighth grader's future. David chose to write and declare my future in front of everyone. After he called me Beano and said, I mean Ruben, he said, "Because of fate he will be great, in politics he will undergo and become the President of Mexico." How about that! The real Beano, David gave me one last shot as he sent me into the future. I had called him Beano for almost two years and teased him about having a missing front tooth that turned out to be just a pinto bean skin covering his front tooth. His send off for me was hilarious and quite clever.

By the end of the eighth grade, I had made some good friends at St. Matthews. It was sad to leave a school where I was a big fish in a small pond. After our graduation ceremony, we were treated with a celebration party at the rectory. It was fun to dance with my sort of girlfriend to the song, "My Girl." The chaperones at our party kept an eye on us like they were guarding the Hope diamond. The year was 1966 and the Motown sound was fabulous. I know eighth-grade boys are not supposed to cry, but I shed a tear that night because I knew a special time in my life was over.

*****

After eighth grade, I lost track of my best friend Jimmy Vaughn as we went to different high schools. About five years later, he hung around with some bad company that decided to rob a hotel at gunpoint, and he ended up with a prison sentence. He was killed while incarcerated. I heard this terrible news while I was in the Navy, and my drive home from San Diego was my *time to mourn*. At his service, I saw Jimmy's mom, and she said, "Ruben the rabbit, it is so good to see you!" She put her fingers by her ears, but she did not give me the buckteeth look as we both wept like babies. She had lost her only son… it was our *time to weep*.

****

I felt good about leaving St. Matthew's as I would attend St. Mary's High School and get to play football for a perennial State Champ. My future was set, but God had other plans for me.

Barrio lesson #15 Working in the onion fields is not something I want to permanently do.

CHAPTER 16

LEFT BEHIND IN EAST LA

My ears heard the words like gunshots, but there was no place for them to land in my mind or heart. My father had just told his elderly parents he was going back to Phoenix without me. I thought I was on a weekend trip to Los Angeles to check on my grandparents. I expected to be home by Monday so I could enjoy the summer of 1966 before starting high school. Before I could protest about not wanting to stay, my father dragged me into one of the small bedrooms so his parents would not hear or see what they might interpret as disrespect. He told me I had no choice in the matter, and he stormed out of the room. His words seemed to ricochet like a pinball inside of me bouncing from my ears to my heart and to my brain. I was devastated as I heard his car struggling to go up the steep hill on Woolwine Drive as he left without saying goodbye.

There was a hurricane of emotions inside of me trying to make sense of this. My mind screamed, "Why?" while my heart tried to hide deeper in my chest. My throat burned with a bitter taste of anger and abandonment. My father was gone. I had no clothes except for what I was wearing. I had no clue how long I had to stay in the heart of East LA. As I laid in bed, hot tears rolled past my cheeks and into my ears. This kind of pain has no place inside a thirteen-year-old boy. I went from the Phoenix barrio (frying pan) into the East LA City Terrace barrio (fire).

After my father left, I spent a couple of hours in my new bedroom. I was confused and couldn't figure out why my father would leave me. I wasn't sure when or if I would go back home. Why me? I thought: There are other cousins my age and older that live in this area that can take care of them. My emotions ran amuck, and I felt betrayed and abandoned. I'm sure it was nothing like what Jesus felt when He was betrayed by Judas and abandoned by His other disciples. Think about how badly Peter must have felt after he denied the Lord. Peter betrayed himself and could not acknowledge he had spent the last three years with Jesus.

My uncle (Tio Teyo) walked in and told me, "Crying is for girls; if you want to cry, I'll give you something to cry about!" He was a hard-core vato, an OG (original gangster). He reminded me of a young Paul Newman with a broken nose. He was always impeccably groomed and drove a beautiful Buick Riviera with a custom paint job. He referred to himself as the Robin Hood of the barrio. He would steal from the rich and give to the poor. Looking past his tattered appearance, there was a hint of kindness in his sad eyes.

Those first nights with my grandparents were long and I had trouble sleeping. I could hear the faint sound of Mexican music late into the night. On one of those first nights, I got up and went into the living room. I was surprised to see my tata (grandfather) awake. He told me about how life was when he was a boy in Jalisco, Mexico. He said, "It was beautiful en el Canon de Gonzales (in Gonzales canyon)." He said he hated leaving there in the early 1900s as his family was fleeing the terror caused by Pancho Villa. He talked about his older brother Victor being killed in the US Army during World War I. He looked sad when he told me his mother changed and remained bitter after that. He told me her bitterness was toward the US government. After my great uncle was killed, the United States did not recognize him as a legal citizen.

During that first week with my grandparents, I went to the corner drugstore and bought my father a card for his June 13th birthday. I even mailed it special delivery. It was my way of checking if he still loved me. There was no way I could call home because long-distance charges were too expensive. My mother sent me a letter about a week later and told me how furious she was when she heard about my father's unilateral decision to leave me there. She told me she knew it was a big change for me and would get me home as soon as she could. Her letter helped soften the constant lump in my throat and gave me the *hope* I needed.

"Now faith is confidence in what we *hope* for and assurance about what we do not see" (Hebrews 11:1).

My dad's youngest brother (Tio Ralph) showed up over the first weekend. He immediately took me to the huge Sears store located near downtown Los Angeles. He bought me a couple of three packs of Fruit of the Loom V-neck T-shirts and briefs. He also spent time with me outside that first day. He brought over two baseball gloves and a baseball, and we played catch on the sidewalk next to the house. Tio Ralph looked like a younger version of my father and even smelled like him. He had no idea how much that first game of catch meant to me. He even got into a catcher's stance and told me to throw him my hardest pitch as he waited for the ball coming at him from a six percent upgrade due to the hill the property sat on.

One of my daily duties was to go to the grocery store for my grandmother. She only spoke Spanish and was showing early signs of Alzheimer's but I thought she was just whacko. Our typical, daily conversation would go like this (in Spanish):

My nana said, "I want you to buy some rice, tomato sauce, and bacon."

I would repeat back what she wanted.

She would then say, "Keep this money deep in your pocket; don't stop to talk to anyone and be quick."

I would then turn quickly and tap-dance down the nineteen stairs and head downhill to the alley toward City Terrace Market. The store was located on City Terrace Drive and sat parallel to Interstate 10, better known as the San Bernardino Freeway. I ran to and from the store as fast as I could. When I got back to the house, I proudly displayed the rice, tomato sauce, and bacon.

Nana looked at it and screamed, "This is not what I wanted; I told you to bring potatoes, beans, and ground beef." She looked at me as if I was from Jupiter, and I felt like I was stuck in the twilight zone.

She would then say, "Ven aquí" which means "come here." She would then rap me on the head with her small knuckles. It didn't hurt me physically, but it bruised my already-demoralized frame of mind. The next day when I took her order for the groceries, I had her show me what she wanted and lined up the items on the kitchen countertop. I told her not to move them until I returned, and then, when I returned, we played match game. This method didn't always work because sometimes she put things away and then I heard those dreaded words of "Ven aquí."

There was one occasion when I went to the store and two rival gangs were about to rumble in the alley. I stayed back to watch when all a sudden I saw three police cars with lights on get to the scene. The gangbangers dropped their weapons and scattered. The police followed them in their vehicles. I was able to pick up a couple of switch blades, a heavy chain, and some brass knuckles. Later that day, I hid these items in the basement. Unfortunately for me, my Tio Teyo found my stash and scolded me for bringing those things to the house. He told me if I ever got involved in any gangs, he would personally beat the crap out of me and my homies. That reminds me of a joke, "What did the vato say after his house fell on him during the earthquake?" Answer, "Get off of me, Holmes!"

I was homesick and spent much of my day gardening with my grandfather. There were lots of snails on the damp, old sidewalk that split the middle of his backyard. My tata grew peaches, avocados, jalapeños, and tomatoes. He liked to repeatedly say daily that in Jalisco, Mexico, his garden was ten times bigger and full of Monarch butterflies. He told me my nana was sick in the head, but I did not fully understand what he meant.

One night my grandfather asked me to come outside to his garden. It was dark and full of shadows everywhere I looked. He looked at me intensely and asked me what I heard. I told him I could hear the cars on the freeway and the sound of crickets and frogs. His eyes got wide and he said, "If you didn't hear these sounds, you could hear the souls in purgatory crying!" I had chills and goose bumps all the way to my scalp. He took me inside so we could pray to his San Martin de Porres statue for the souls in purgatory. It was somewhat spooky at the time. It is how he was taught;

unfortunately, I have never read about purgatory in the Bible. Look at what it says about statues in Psalm 115 verses 4–8: "But their idols are silver and gold, made by human hands. They have mouths, but cannot speak, eyes, but cannot see. They have ears, but cannot hear, noses, but cannot smell. They have hands but cannot feel, feet, but cannot walk, nor can they utter a sound with their throats. Those who make them will be like them, and so will all who trust in them." I feel badly now that I know better. Back at my tata's wake, I snuck a replica of St. Martin into his coffin. I repeat, there is only one way to the Father and that is through His son, Jesus.

My cousin Billy lived nearby in the projects. He was two months younger than me and came to visit daily on his bicycle. It was his job to go to the grocery store for nana before my arrival. He laughed when he asked me if I went to the store and then got ackees afterward. He named the rap on the head ackees because it sounded like the word aquí.

Early one morning while I was in a deep sleep, my cousin Billy came over and woke me up. He told me if I did not get up, he was going to give me some ackees. He began rapping me on the head and I warned him to stop. He did it again, so I sprung out of bed and delivered a perfect 1-2 knuckle sandwich right on his nose.

He began bleeding and ran out of the house with blood splattered on his dingy, white T-shirt. That evening, his mom, my aunt Lilly, called my Tio Teyo to let him know I had made Billy's nose bleed. My tio told her he would call her right back. He then gave me instructions when he called her back to yell like I was getting hit every time his belt hit the bed mattress. He called my aunt back so she could hear the punishment he was inflicting on me. After he got off the phone, my tio wanted to know why I punched Billy. When I told him what had happened, he said, "If he does that again, you hit that little SOB, but this time don't make him leak (bleed)." After that incident, my tio gained a new sense of respect from me and vice versa. From Romans 13:7, "Give to everyone what you owe them: ... if you owe taxes, pay taxes... if you owe *respect*, then respect."

After that incident, I used to ride with my Tio Teyo in his car and everyone in the City Terrace barrio knew him. He was not around very much, but even without him there, his reputation provided me an invisible hedge of protection in this rough neighborhood. He gave me the street name of Big Shode (Mexican slang for shorty). I told him I wanted to be like him when I grew up. He quickly replied, "Ni lo mande Dios!" (loosely translated means heaven forbid).

One evening my tio came home from work and gruffly inquired, "Hey, Big Shode, do you know how to fix bikes?" I told him yes, and with a gleam in his eye, he stepped outside and brought in a large box containing a bicycle. He said, "Here, put it together!" So, I began to assemble the bike right there in the small living room. It was a brand-new blue stingray bike with a banana seat. When I finished assembling it, he just looked at me. I awkwardly asked him who the bike was for. He gruffly said, "Who do you think?" and I mumbled I don't know.

He said, "It's yours!" and I almost hit the floor in shock. I hugged him and thanked him profusely. I asked him where he got it from, and he said, "Ask me no questions and I'll tell you no lies." It was by far my best day in East LA.

For the rest of the summer, I rode all over the hills of East LA with my cousin Billy. We would ride our bikes to visit our Bonilla cousins in El Sereno. It was always an adventure to ride our bikes because of the hills, traffic, dogs, and no GPS. My advantage was being street savvy from my paper punk days. Billy and I were fearless as we went to the highest hill and then raced down the narrow streets. We were fortunate not to have any accidents, but one time we had to "lay down" our bikes and slide under an eighteen-wheel trailer that was not there the day before. One time my young cousin Ruben begged me for a ride. During a 180 degree Batman turn, he got his foot stuck in the spoke of the back tire—ouch! My other cousin Shaver always wanted a ride on my bike, but I would not let him even sit on the banana seat because he was not potty trained.

My nana restricted my bike riding to two hours per day, one hour in the morning and another hour in the late afternoon. This included the time it took to go to the store for her. I really resented her rules. My breaking point came when she changed her mind at the last minute and did not allow me to go to Disneyland with my Tio Bonilla and family. My

Tia Terri tried to convince her as we had made plans to go to Disneyland for several weeks. I was livid, and that night while lying in bed, I made up my mind to run (ride) away back to Phoenix.

I started collecting jars with lids for water and found an old Army canteen that my uncle used during the Korean War. My new friend Sleepy gave me some old motorcycle bags to carry stuff. I studied the map at the gas station near City Terrace Market. It was four hundred and forty-three miles to Phoenix. If I followed Interstate 10, it would lead me home. I figured I could ride forty miles a day and make it home in about eleven days. I planned to travel at night so I could go undetected and avoid the desert heat. I planned to eat by going into grocery stores and pretend that I was shopping. It was my intention to make and eat sandwiches and leave the store unnoticed. I circled the date August 8, 1966, on the calendar, the date to leave and make it home one day before my birthday.

But before I could ride my bike back home ...... God had a better plan for me.

In Jeremiah 29:11, it says, "'For I know the *plans* I have for you,' declares the Lord, '*plans* to prosper you and not harm you, *plans* to give you hope and a future.'"

Paternal grandparents Refugio Figueroa and Francisco Gonzales
Photo date: approximately 1922

Barrio lesson # 16 Bloom where you are planted.

CHAPTER 17

FROM BARRIO TO SEMINARY

My plan to ride my bike to Phoenix did not happen because God came to the rescue. Sometime during the summer of 1966, I had contacted my friend Joe from St. Matthew's. Joe had been accepted in Dominguez Seminary so he could become a priest. Prior to the beginning of the next school year, he had a pre-visit to the seminary. Long story... short, I was invited to go on a weekend visit. I remember the priest by the name of Frank Ambrosi driving up the steep hill on Woolwine Drive to pick me up. Joe and two other boys from East LA were inside the small station wagon. The priest broke the ice by asking me, "Has anyone ever told you how handsome you are?" I nervously answered no, and he said, "Don't worry, I don't think anyone ever will." We all laughed and were on our way to the seminary in Compton.

The other two boys in the car were named Frank and Manuel. Frank was street-smart and quickly made a pact with me in the car. He said if any of the other kids give us trouble at the seminary, we will stick together, and we shook on it. Frank was quick to recognize the tough neighborhood where they picked me up and figured I would make a strong ally.

The seminary was in the Dominguez Hills area and the grounds were gorgeous. There were lots of persimmon trees and a huge swimming pool. It had ample room for fields used for baseball, football, and soccer. The food during the weekend was outstanding and I loved it there. In a matter of a weekend, I transformed from near thug to seminarian as I decided to become a priest. This was not well thought out, but it got me back to Phoenix so I could get ready for the fast-approaching school year at the seminary.

It was odd getting back home as I was now a church celebrity at Our Lady of Fatima. Various people from the church gave donations to off-set tuition costs plus room and board. My brothers' friends treated me differently and would no longer curse in front of me. Prior to leaving for the seminary, I had second thoughts about going, but the avalanche of support and well wishes was unstoppable. So, I became a Claretian Missionary Postulate at the ripe age of fourteen. It was a hasty decision, and as I reflect on this, I cite, "It is better to not to make a vow than to make one and not fulfill it" (Ecclesiastes 5:5).

Since my parents could not afford the tuition, I had to offset the costs by scrubbing pots and pans. My friend Juan worked alongside me after every lunch and dinner. We worked furiously because our cleaning time was during the time other seminarians had free time for playing sports. Juan is still my friend on Facebook today as his brother Joseph got married to my cousin Conchita. It was difficult work, but I could not complain as I had taken the vow of humility. As a Claretian Missionary Postulate, I could add CMP behind my name. It should have been CMS for Claretian Missionary Slave; it was jacked up.

We did not do any bible study at the seminary. There were days where silence was declared, and we were told to go "meditate." I had no idea what that meant, but my behavior was to be as solemn as I could be and I should stay out of trouble. Almost immediately, we were given a card with St. Anthony Claret. It really bothered me when I found out later in life what I was taught in the seminary about salvation (going to heaven) was not true. One of the first teachings I received was if I prayed the prayer on the back of St. Anthony Claret's novena card, I would be guaranteed the right to enter heaven. Saying this prayer, along with receiving communion on nine consecutive first Fridays of the month, was my ticket and fireproof admission into the Pearly Gates. What a crock! At the time, it made me feel good because I was convinced I had earned salvation.

I feel very strongly against this false teaching and want to emphasize: we only go to heaven because "God loves us so much; He gave us His only son who died for us. Whoever believes in Him will not perish but have eternal life." It is not about Jesus plus something, like confessing to a priest, burning candles, spending time in purgatory, and rubbing a Buda or beads. Jesus is the Way, the Truth and the Life… period.

My favorite teacher, Mr. Williams, taught our English class. We (freshmen) used to call him Willy, and he did not like that nickname. Somehow, we found out Mr. Williams had a girlfriend named Madeline and we would make comments about their relationship. For example, we would ask if he and Madeline were going out that weekend. He would turn red and politely tell us talking about her was not part of the curriculum.

He wore shirts that were heavily starched, and he constantly tugged at his shirt collar and tie, stretched his neck, and rotated his head to get relief. One day, we plotted that during his class, at the fifteen-minute mark to the second, all of us would simultaneously tug at our shirts, stretch out necks, and rotate our heads. Mr. Williams did a double take and took a gulp of water when he saw forty students do this in unison. In fifteen minutes, we did it again, and this time he screamed, "Cut that out!" It was hilarious for us, but it must have stunned him to see this happen.

There was Father Schneider who looked like Archie Bunker and taught us algebra. He would wrinkle his face up and liked to say "Oh, a wise guy, aye!" He would quote Popeye by saying, "I may not be a physicist, but I know what matters." Ben, who was from San Antonio and looked like Alfred E. Neuman from *Mad* magazine, could imitate him the best. There were four boys from San Antonio that enrolled with me as freshmen at the seminary. Lorenzo, aka Virgin Ears, was the only one from our class of forty students to be ordained as a priest. The four guys from San Antonio had to ride the Greyhound bus for thirty-six hours to get to the seminary.

The seminary had its own lingo and we used words like "spazz," "bennies," and "I'm divin'" in a sarcastic way to show enthusiasm. Our symbol to tell someone to grow up was to put your finger and thumb about an inch apart and show it to the person you wanted to settle down. Benny was the nickname for a freshman and was assigned to a sophomore who provided guidance. My sophomore sponsor was a guy named Fessler who spoke with a lisp and would say his last name was Feffler. I used to make fun of him until he slugged me with a good punch to the stomach. He apologized and begged me not to tell anyone. He bribed me by giving me his donut that was freshly made. Give me a donut and my lips are sealed.

We went to outings as a school on two rented cattle trucks. Some of the students had a difficult time climbing into the truck. We sometimes had spit wads flying from one truck to the other. Back then, there was a cigarette commercial that advertised, show us your Lark pack. We would hold a sign out and people would show us their various cigarette packs and honk. One of the most memorable outings was going to the snow at Mt. Baldy. This was my first time in the snow and I quickly mastered riding a toboggan. I loved playing in the snow and have always had the desire to snow ski. Is a sixty-seven-year old like I am now too late to learn? To be determined.

My most memorable games during that freshman year happened when we played football against the sophomores. There was a guy named Norwood who was supposed to be the fastest guy at the seminary. During a fiercely competitive game against the sophomore class, Norwood was on his way to a game-winning touchdown when he got rundown and tackled from behind by the Ruben the rabbit. All the faculty and fellow seminarians were at the game, and everyone was shocked when I brought down Norwood at full speed. We won the game that day and finally beat the sophomores. After that, I had the unofficial title of being the fastest kid in the school. He always challenged me to race him in a dash, but I preferred to keep my new unofficial title by not racing him. I knew he was faster than me, but with the game on the line and when my adrenalin kicked in, he was toast. I did the Edwin walk (loose, confident from da hood walk) for several days afterward. Edwin is my grandson now that walks the walk and laughs when I attempt to imitate him with my rheumatoid-infested right knee.

During the weekends the local kids were able to go home. Occasionally, my uncle Ralph would have me take a taxi to his work on Friday. I would spend the weekend at his house, and he took me to several Dodger baseball games. The seminary sometimes held open houses and I had regular visits from my Tio Junior, Tia Weenie (mom's sister), Tio Panchito (mom's brother), and all my young Godinez cousins. Those are wonderful memories as they spent the day and we ate "picnic" food. My Tio Panchito would always pass me a couple of dollars so I could buy something to eat from the seminary store.

One weekend, my Tio Ruben and Tia Terri took me and two of my classmates from Phoenix, Joe and Ernie, to their house in El Sereno. While we were enjoying a pancake breakfast, my Tio Ruben asked one of us to pass the "surp," and the three of us giggled. We used the word surp instead of syrup several times during that meal. I loved spending time at their house because my tia was always cooking up a storm. I used to call my tio "Tornillo" because that was the name of the town he grew up in near El Paso, TX.

One of the guys in my class named Craig was a ventriloquist. He had a puppet named Cletus that was rude and extremely disrespectful. Cletus was always saying things that were politically correct. He made fun of Brother Norbert's nose and the size of his feet. There were times at the end of his shows that Cletus did not want to get put away in his box. Craig was brilliant in the way he made it look like Cletus was alive and yelled to let him out from inside the box. In a way, Cletus was kind of creepy but very entertaining. Craig could make Cletus sing at the same time he drank water.

****

I saw Craig's brother on an airplane trip about thirty years later. I just happened to notice the name Woolgar on his boarding pass. It was sometime after November 1999 as I had already been born again. Although I had never met Craig's brother, we connected because I recognized their unusual last name. Craig's brother was a Jesus freak, and we talked on the plane about the seminary's take on Salvation. His brother talked about Cletus and then did his best ventriloquist imitation. He went into a Cletus routine on the plane and was saying loudly, "Dominguez Seminary teaches false doctrine." We had a fabulous time on that airplane ride. Other passengers must have thought we had too much to drink with all our laughter. It was much like at the day of Pentecost when the Apostles were filled with the Holy Spirit and began to speak in other tongues as the Spirit enabled them. This story can be found in Acts Chapter 2. This story goes on to say this about those who heard them: "Amazed and perplexed they asked one another, 'What does this mean?' Some, however, made fun of them and said, 'They have had too much wine'" (Acts 2: 12–13).

****

During the summer of 1967, I went home and worked at Legend City. The amusement park was being refurbished, and we were part of a work crew to get it ready for reopening. Joe's dad got us employment there and our primary job was to chip paint. It was a summer job and we sweated all day and went home with paint chips stuck on our eyelids. We went home looking like a science project gone wrong with a scent of funk.

One of the things that surprised me when I went home that summer was that my three sisters had turned the furniture padding I used as a cover all my childhood into what they called the "popcorn blanket." In an earlier chapter, I mentioned Sada had given this to me with all his heart as the house was cold. I must point out when you give, like to a mission, you have no idea how far your gift will go. My sisters benefitted

108

from Sada's gift to me as they spread this blanket on the floor and spread popcorn on it as Lupe babysat her younger siblings. After they ate the popcorn, they shook "the popcorn blanket" and used it as their blanket. This now explains why their hair was always so shiny and had a popcorn scent. LOL.

Prior to beginning my second year at the seminary, I visited my grandparents. My Tio Teyo drove me to the seminary in his immaculate Buick Riviera to Compton. On the way, he pulled over to help a wino who was in front of a liquor store begging for money. The wino approached the car and asked my tio for two dollars for bus fare. My tio was annoyed and told him to come closer and pretended he couldn't hear him. My tio grabbed him by the collar and slapped him a couple of time. My tio said, "No me heches mentiras, quieres comprar vino!" (Don't lie to me, you want to buy wine). The stunned wino apologized and said he really needed a drink so he could stop shaking. My tio gave him two dollars, told him to buy some "Mad Dog 20/20," and said, "I want the first drink, Holmes!" When the wino came out, my tio took a big swig as the thirsty wino watched. My tio laughed and asked me if I wanted a drink as part of priest training. I declined and it was a quiet ride to the seminary because of his cutting remark.

When we arrived at 18127 S. Alameda, my tio stopped once he entered the seminary grounds. He said, "Hey Big Shode, are you sure you want to go to school here?" I hesitated and he said, "Just give the word, and I'll drive you back to Phoenix, quick!" Thoughts of returning home flashed through my mind, but I told him this is where I need to be. I looked back sadly after he dropped me off and I saw him drive away.

My friend Ernie (RIP) was part of a trio that called themselves the Dominguez Brass. Their three-piece band played lots of Herb Alpert songs like "Tijuana Taxi" and "The Lonely Bull." They were talented; Ernie played the trumpet and his brother Ricky played the sliding trombone. Their parents were my parents' compadres as they baptized my brother Ernie who is named after Mr. Quiroz.

During my second year at the seminary, I continued to do extra work to pay off my tuition. This time, I was put in charge of the work team responsible for washing all the plates, glasses, and silverware after every meal. It was a real pain to round up the five or six guys so we could finish quickly. I learned some valuable techniques for motivating slackers; sometimes I would use praise, make threats, give extra work, or peer pressure. Although it was hard, it provided a platform for preparing me for working over thirty-five years in USPS management.

During that second year, I really excelled in soccer. My fried Manuel from East LA showed me some ways to handle the ball in game situations. He was so agile on his feet that he could ascend stairs by kicking his legs forward like doing a Russian dance on his way up. He tried to show me how to do this, but I could only do it going down the stairs. Manuel was the best player on the team, but I was not far behind him. Our team went undefeated, and we beat one of the teams 13-0. One time we played against a team from one of the local detention facilities. They were rough and used bad language while making fun of us "padresitos" (little priests). I had to go to confession later that week because I also had some words for them that a seminarian should not use. Coach/Brother Marciel pulled me out of the game and told to settle me down. I was frustrated with all their holding and unnecessary bumping. After I got back into the game, I was able to score a goal from about thirty yards out. We won that game and gained the respect of the prisoners

We played in South Torrance in our first game of the playoffs and we won. Tio Ralph was at that game and told me he was super proud of me. He was also at the quarter final game the following week against San Gabriel when we lost 4-1. He comforted me and pointed out our school only had eighty students while San Gabriel had several hundred students. He said, "You can't always win, but never give up the 'ganas' (desire) to want to win." He went on to say, "When you lose the ganas to win is when you lose." My soccer coach told me I could probably make it to All CIF (California Interscholastic Federation) as a forward in the upcoming year if I practiced hard during the summer. He was extremely disappointed when he found out I would not return for my junior year. He tried to convince me several times by calling me in Phoenix during the summer of 1968… by then I was Gone-zales!

On a sad note, my Tio Ralph died within ten years in his late thirties. It is my understanding he was having a problem with high blood pressure but continued to drink. I never confirmed this and don't want to; there was a rumor he was taking things to keep him awake when he drank. God bless you Tio Ralph, thanks for playing catch with me on the side of my grandparents' house. Note: this made me shed tears as I wrote it.

Barrio lesson # 17 Don't decide to become a priest over the weekend.

CHAPTER 18

A STEP BACK INTO THE BARRIO

My decision to leave the seminary was well more thought out than my "one weekend visit" decision to enter it. During my sophomore year, I was treated to a boxing match by my cousin Baby Saw; he lost the coin flip to my Tio Teyo and paid for the three of us. They picked me up for the weekend and took me to see a championship fight at the LA Olympic Auditorium between heavyweights Floyd Patterson and Jerry Quarry. Some of the fights among fans had more action than some of the prefights leading to the main event. We cheered for Patterson, but the much younger Quarry won the fight.

During that weekend, I offered to wash my Tio's car in front of my grandparent's house. A young lady approached me as I was cleaning the car. At first, I did not recognize her as she said, "Dude, (that's what the kids from the block called me) they must feed you good at that priest school because you grew a lot in a year." She was one of the kids I hung around with the year prior. She had transformed into some serious eye candy, and it made me nervous instantly. I mumbled something like, "You don't look so bad yourself." She told me about her upcoming quinceañera (fifteen-year-old coming out party) and asked me if I wanted to be her escort. I told her I would have to check if it was permissible by the seminary. She chuckled and said in a sassy manner, "If you ever don't want to be a priest, you know where I live." She smiled and I liked the way she was looking at me. She said goodbye and started her glide (smooth walk) down the street. I was hypnotized by her gentle sway and noticed the woman curves she was developing. My tio came out of the house and broke my trance by yelling, "Que miras bobo!" (means what are you staring at; bobo is slang which means something like googly eyes). He was laughing and after I wiped the drool off my face, I rapidly continued washing his car. My thoughts were spinning, and I thanked God for all that good seminary food. I felt my name could be Daniel changed to Belteshazzar in Daniel Chapter 1. Read it, and you'll like the story.

When I returned to the seminary, it was hard to concentrate as I day-dreamed about going to the quinceañera. My final decision not to return to the seminary came during the summer break. Two of my cousins invited me to a movie with Raquel Welch in it. She looked stunning in the movie and my fifteen-year-old thoughts were on her constantly. My male hormones were in full bloom, and I knew I could not commit to a life of celibacy. Sorry priesthood, girls win, I'm out!

One of the first things I did when I got back home from the seminary was to get a job at the nearby grocery store. My cousin Eddie worked there, and their family was getting ready to move to California. Eddie asked me if I wanted to have interview for his job at Moe's Food Fair Market. I was excited about working and getting paid for it directly. The store was located on the corner of 19th Avenue and Buckeye Road. It was close to the Coffelt projects and a walking distance to our house. The store was in desperate need of a makeover with a complete steam cleaning. It had a unique smell; I guess you could call it storeatosis. After I was inter-viewed by the produce manager named Roy at 10 am, I began working that same day. Roy's hands trembled and we used to say he was good at chucking onions. Chucking onions is a process of removing the dry, excessive onion skins to make them more presentable for sale.

This store provided lots of adventures for me like being on a roller coaster with a wobbly wheel. I will devote a couple of chapters to capture some of the things that happened while I worked there for three years prior to joining the Navy. For example, during my first meeting with the assistant manager, he made me an interesting offer. He told me if I paid him fifty dollars per paycheck, he would look the other way while I "grocery shopped." Being freshly out of the seminary, I declined, and he was upset and told me he would fire me on the spot if he caught me stealing anything.

There was always some kind of commotion or crisis going on at Moe's Food Fair Market. On one of my first days at the store, a black dude, probably in his late twenties, robbed the store. The store manager called out on the intercom system, "The store has been robbed and we have to catch him before he gets away!" He sounded frantic, and, in no time, I joined about four or five male coworkers on a chase to get him. Since I was in top condition from playing soccer at the seminary, I caught up with the robber in the alley near Buck's store. When I looked behind me, none of my coworkers were there as they had tired out. I don't remember picking up a large rock to defend myself. I was surprised when the robber turned and growled at me, "Boy, whatcha gonna do with that rock!" I was about ten feet from him and felt sheer terror saturating my sixteen-year-old body. I was like a statue and I could not talk. Then, by the grace of God, my unexpected guardian angel showed up. A man stepped out of a gate from his backyard and had a rifle pointed at the robber. He screamed, "Don't you do anything to that boy!" My God-appointed protector held him at gunpoint until the police arrived. One of the promises in the Bible is found in Psalm 91:1" "For He will command His angels concerning you to guard you in all your ways." My coworkers admired my courage, but it was the most stupid thing I have ever done. I used to worry that the robber would come back to get me for chasing him.

Shortly after the robbery, a new owner bought the store and named it Carlito's Market. The new owner was a rich dairy farmer, and his name was Charlie. He changed the name to Carlito's to fit into the barrio, even though he was a gringo. There had been prevalent misconduct in the store with internal loss occurring daily. After the new owner bought the store, I was one of the employees that remained employed under the new management. My "brown Bro" was let go, along with five other coworkers. The new owner brought in a new manager named Omar. He was easygoing, but his exterior was burly and gruff. He gave me lots of "consejos" (fatherly advice), and I quickly established a strong friendship with him. He hired a couple of my friends based on my recommendation.

One of them was Coop, who was a close friend of mine from Our Lady of Fatima. We made our first communion together. There used to be a bus stop-type bench in front of the store that we referred to as the wino bench. One day Coop's dad sat innocently on the bench while waiting for him. I made fun of Coop by telling him, "At least my dad does not sit on the wino bench." The wino bench was the hangout spot for a menagerie of characters that drank out of a brown bag.

Coop and I thought we were slick and referred to Omar as Ramo. As we stocked shelves, we would say, "Work hard or Ramo is gonna get you!" One day Omar laughed, and said he knew Ramo was Omar spelled backward. Omar once asked Coop and I to chase a wino that had jacked a bottle of wine. We chased him across the empty field, and he banged on the back door of his unit. He yelled, "Abre la puerta!" which means open the door. We took the bottle of wine away from him and tossed it into Coop's 1948 Dodge. Omar asked us if we caught the wino and we said he got away. I know it was wrong to lie, but we were in our junior year of high school and alcohol was a challenge to obtain... for a little while.

We somehow got the brilliant idea to place beer inside a large box under the concealment of lettuce trimmings. We would place the box by the back door, and at lunch time we would take the "lettuce drink" leaves to our make-believe rabbits. At home my mother had given up the fight to stop my father from drinking on weekends and had joined him. Her advice to me as I wanted to partake with my two older brothers was, "If you are going to drink, at least learn how to hold it!" So, I did. My parents approved my drinking at age seventeen to coincide with my oldest brother's return from Vietnam.

There was also a butcher from Tennessee that invited me to drink a "toddy" of bourbon almost nightly prior to going home.

He always kept his daily pint of bourbon stashed away in the meat locker. When my coworkers asked me why I drank with him, I would laugh and tell my friends, "Jay the butcher does not like to drink alone." It was the start of a low point in my life but that's what I did. Did you know that Noah drank? "Noah, a man of the soil, proceeded to plant a vineyard. When he drank some of its wine, he became drunk and lay uncovered inside his tent" (Genesis 9: 20–21).

It wasn't long after I started working when one of my female friends I knew through grammar school came to visit me at the store. At the time I did not have much interaction with young ladies since that was not part of the seminary curriculum. She was dressed nicely, and I was surprised at how attractive she had become. The way she was dressed was way too nice for Carlito's Market. She was wearing a white dress and looked like she was on her way to an Easter Sunday service. This was during the summer in Phoenix when temperatures average about a thousand degrees. She welcomed me back and wasted no time in asking me if I had a girlfriend. She proceeded to tell me she did not have a boyfriend. It was awkward for me and I let her know I would keep my eye out to help her find a boyfriend. My comment ended that conversation abruptly, and she made a quick exit from the store. I distinctly remember the fast-clicking noise from her heels as she left.

When I told my brother Richard about it, he let me know how dumb I was. He said she was one of the most popular girls at Phoenix Union High School and all the guys were always trying to get her attention. Even though she was gorgeous, and I knew she was a good girl, I was not anywhere ready to get involved with someone. It was a real culture shock for me to go from the protected, isolated, sterile seminary environment to the hard-core, inner city Carl Hayden High School and Carlito's Market. Richard encouraged me to seek her out, but it did not feel right for me. Since I had known her from kindergarten to sixth grade at Jackson School, it felt like she was more like my sister than a potential love connection.

One day while I was working in the produce area, I saw a man with no legs on a wheelchair approaching the store on the opposite side of Buckeye

Road. He seemed to be having a difficult time moving his wheelchair on the field between the projects and the store. As I watched, this no-legged man went down a cemented, unfinished driveway and fell backward from his wheelchair to the ground. He was squirming on the ground like a short, wounded caterpillar. I quickly sprinted from the store to pick him up and asked him if he was okay. He did not answer, and I figured he was discombobulated by his fall. I dusted him off and was surprised at how easily I could lift him up and place him back on his wheelchair. I helped him get across the street to the store side and went back inside the store. I kept my eye on him and he turned to cross the street again toward the projects. The man with no legs managed to flip his wheelchair again and fell hard to the ground. He squirmed in the manner of a cut fishing worm before you place it on the hook. I ran to him again and scolded him, "What are you doing?" I picked him up roughly and put him back on his wheelchair. I took him across Buckeye and a police car pulled up next to us. One of the officers said, "Looks like Romeo has been drinking and is up to his old tricks." They put his wheelchair into their patrol car and told me they would take him home. I went back to the store shaking my head in disbelief; the man with no legs was drunk.

There was a fiery Italian man that worked at Carlito's. His nickname was Kumbati because that's what he called everyone. I think kumbati is an Italian word that means comrade. He was intense and had a defective-looking eyeball. The pupil on his left eye looked like a clear straw you could follow deep into his eye. It was weird and difficult for me to hold a conversation with him. Sometimes when I talked with him, he would yell, "Quit looking at my eye!" I would always try to sneak in a peek at his eye, but it was impossible, and he would get annoyed. When I got to know him better, I asked him once if I could get a good hard look at his eye without him going berserk. I explained to him if I could examine his eye thoroughly, I would get the curiosity out of my system. He agreed but cut off my examination of his albino eye pupil prematurely because I asked, "Does it hurt?" Kumbati responded with his favorite saying, "If I had a dime for every time someone asked me about my eye, I wouldn't be working at this dump!"

I developed the ability to very carefully make eye jokes. For example, if there was a potential shoplifter in the store, I told him I needed his help to keep an eye on them. When a new female cashier was hired to work at the store, I would tell her that Kumbati had an eye on her. Once this new employee cashier caught on, she thought it was really funny.

Kumbati was a strange puppy and would go through his nightly checklist prior to going home. He would say, "Let's see, I got my coat, I got my wallet, I got my keys, I got my spectacles, and I got my testicles." He would then grab his crotch and leave. He needed a good session of kum-by-yah with a couple of servings of chamomile tea. In the words of my daughter-in-law Misti, "he was a hot mess."

The store would get crazy busy when customers received their welfare checks. We had four cashier stations, and each one of them was overloaded with food on the third of the month for about three or four hours. By this time, I had become very proficient at being a cashier. During one of the busiest, most chaotic days, one of the carryouts named Johnny ran a shopping cart into the bubblegum machine and shattered the glass. There were gumballs rolling everywhere in the heaviest foot traffic areas. To make matters worse, Coop picked up a gumball and threw it at Johnny. He hit Johnny directly in the eye. and Johnny made a big fuss over how much his eye hurt.

Now during our most busy day, we were short a carry out, who was crying in the back room and we still had a million gumballs on the floor. Coop and Johnny yelled at each other in front of a packed store, and that moment epitomized what it was like to work there.

Later that same night, I watched Coop pick up a frozen pepperoni pizza that had come out of the box and fallen to the floor when he was bagging groceries. The pizza box had been sliced open on the edge by an erratic box cutter, and the pizza slid out of the opening before Coop put it in the grocery bag. It was like a moment frozen in time to see the customer's pizza and two pepperonis rolling simultaneously on the floor. Coop was quick enough to retrieve the pizza and two pepperonis and put them back into the box without the customer noticing. The customer ended up complimenting Coop for being such an efficient bagger. She had no idea her pepperoni pizza might have a hint of bubblegum flavor after spending time on the floor.

It was a difficult evening as we had to roller skate on gumballs all night. We still made Johnny pick them up since he was the one that broke the gumball dispenser. At the end of the shift, we, including Johnny, laughed about how crazy that night was. We went into the back room and chugged a beer before going home. We threw our empty cans on top of the walk-in produce cooler while Omar was at the front of the store closing out the cash registers.

Barrio lesson #18 Never chase down a person who has just robbed a store.

CHAPTER 19

THE CIRCUS CONTINUES

On a nightly basis at Carlito's, shortly after closing, we had to keep the front area lights on so we can see when sweeping and mopping the entrance area of the store. This gave an appearance that the store was still open. We got annoyed whenever customers arrived at the store after it closed and then expected us to reopen the doors for them. The double doors were made mostly of thick glass and had a locking mechanism that secured both doors in the middle. This left lots of rattle room and created an annoying sound. When customers arrived just after closing, they would sometimes shake the doors with all their strength in disgust. We called these customers LMCs, which stood for last-minute customers. We also called some customers WCs which meant walking complaints.

One night Coop had the task of sweeping and mopping the front area when two large, black women got to the store after closing. As he mopped, they yelled, "Hey Moe's boy!" as they rattled the door. They still referred to the store as Moe's instead of Carlito's. Coop said, "We're closed!" and kept mopping. One of the women said, "Hey Moe's boy, here's two dollars, my baby needs some milk!" She held two dollars between the door opening. Coop just ignored them and continued to mop. The woman now screamed, "Moe's boy, you know you hear us, go and get my baby some @&#*¥ milk!" At this Coop lost it and yelled, "Get out of here, you LMCs, you last-minute coons, the store is closed!" The two women were now furious and asked, "What's your name Moe's boy? We're gonna get you when you get off!" Coop came and told me what had happened and asked me if I could walk with him to his car after we finished cleaning. Coop also asked Omar if he could go out through the back door, but Omar said no. Coop did not tell Omar about the door shaking incident. When we walked out, Coop had "los ojos pelados" (eyes wide and looking in every direction) as he trotted to his car. He drove home using a different route just in case he was being followed.

There were five of us guys from Carl Hayden High School that worked there after school and on weekends. Since I had the most seniority and recommended my coworkers for employment, I was their informal supervisor and team leader. By the time we were seniors, we regularly drank a beer or two in the back room during our work shift. We would dispose of our empty cans by throwing them in the space above one of the walk-in refrigerators. One day Omar called all of us into the back room and showed us a garbage bag of empty beer cans he found above the walk-in refrigerator. He asked us if we knew how these cans got there, and we told him it was probably from the guys that worked here before us. He told us we would be fired if he caught us drinking beer during work. We told him he would never catch us doing that. From that point forward, we were more careful and disposed of the cans by burying them in the box that contained the lettuce trimmings.

Around that time, an older guy named Ben was hired to help with the overall management of the store. He was thin and always full of energy. He reminded me of a confident Barney Fife from *The Andy Griffith Show*. He had lots of ideas on how he would become a millionaire one day. At this point, I was moved from produce into the meat department. Shortly after Ben's arrival, a new product named Right Time beer was launched. It tasted okay and I told Ben about this new flavored beer. After a couple of hours, I saw Ben with a gleam in his eye, and he told me, "I already drank five Right Time beers." It surprised me that Ben would drink at work, even though it was common practice for us.

The next time I saw Ben was about four days later. He showed up at the back door of the store and looked like the star hobo from a horror movie. He had a large knot and scrape on his head from where he had fallen. He was also unshaven and dirty from wearing the same clothes without the benefit of Depends. He begged us to give him a bottle of wine. We told him to sit in the back room and hurried to tell Omar. Omar took him home back to his halfway house and from there he went into detox. We did not know Ben was a reformed alcoholic. I felt like crap and wished there was something I could do for Ben. Too much alcohol is not good for anyone, including me. "Wine is a mocker and beer is a brawler; whoever is lead astray from them is not wise" (Proverbs 20:1).

There was another older man named Jim that came in to assist Omar. He was more of a store greeter and walked around talking to customers. He referred to himself as "old dad," and that's what we called him. He was always encouraging us and told me I had movie star looks. He would tell random customers that I should be in the movies. One time my mother came into the store; he did not know my mom but told her about me needing to go to Hollywood. She wholeheartedly agreed and old dad told me, "See I told you so." Note: My mother would pretend like she did not know me when she shopped (more on this shortly). Old dad encouraged me when I needed it most. He was wise enough to see the potential in me but also recognized my chances of going astray. He planted numerous words of wisdom that I needed to hear. But when you are walking in darkness, you do not understand the Truth. "The wise have eyes in their heads while a fool walks in darkness" (Ecclesiastes 2:14). It's a sad thing when you hear the Truth and don't do anything about it. It's even worse when you are *not* given the chance to find and/or examine the Truth. So, you continue your barrio walk in the dark path of foolishness.

Old dad pointed out girls that he thought were interested in me. There was a cute, healthy young lady that would visit me regularly when I was a meat wrapper. She would buy a whole dill pickle from the large glass container on top of the meat display counter. Old dad would tell me, this girl really loves you. We went out a few times, and she wanted to get serious quicker than I wanted to. Her dad was super strict, and the only time I got to see her was when he was out of town, which wasn't too often. The last time I saw her was after I returned from the Navy which was shortly before I got married. She begged me to spend more time with her, and I probably should have listened to her.

One of the more memorable workers at the store was a butcher from Memphis named Clay. He claimed to be part of Elvis Presley's inner circle of friends. On a couple of occasions when he was a little inebriated, he said he could call Elvis by phone. I told him I did not believe him and wanted to talk to Elvis. He pulled a phone number out of his wallet and dialed. He supposedly reached "the Colonel" that told him Elvis was not home. After that I would sing to him during our closing routine, "You ain't nothing but a hound dog just a crying all the time."

I would tell the butcher from Tennessee to mark up some "dog bones" as T-bone steaks for my mother who remained incognito. We marked a dog bone package with three x's so the customer could present it at the checkout register and not be charged. My brother Papo and cousin Joey picked up some "dog bones" once. They were loud and made fun of how badly the store smelled. The two of them hanging around together brought out the worst in each other.

One of Clay's favorite lines to customers was, "Are you going to eat it here or take it with you?" He would ask this no matter what they were buying, that is, fresh chicken, ground beef, or tripe. He also would ask mainly female customers, "How's yours?" He was implying her private area and would wait for a reaction. He then quickly changed it to, "How are you?" if he saw the customer seemed agitated. He was one, crazy "pelon." Pelon means bald dude.

Omar brought in an assistant manager named Tim Jones. He came in with a micro-management style and immediately began cracking the whip. He told us we would never make it in a real store. He belittled us, and even though we worked extremely hard, he was never pleased. We got tired of him quickly, and I knew we had to change his attitude or change jobs. Tim was a biker wannabe and rolled his short sleeves up to show off his biceps. He had pock marks on his face and a sharp pointed nose. He had slicked back blonde hair and combed the back into a duck-tail. My first step in bringing him down was to challenge him to arm wrestling after the store had closed. I had been working out at home and during PE at school. My coworkers were there to see our arm wrestling at the service desk counter. Much to my surprise, I put his arm down fairly quickly with authority. Johnny screamed in delight when I won. Tim did not know how to act after losing, and I strutted around the store like George Jefferson (from the TV show called *The Jeffersons*).

The next day after our arm wrestling, I made a poster from a piece of cardboard and drew a face on it. I outlined a face that scowled, and for the nose I place a shriveled up "chile guerito" or yellow pepper. Above the sign, I wrote, "Tim Jones—Chili Nose." The guys thought it was hilarious. Johnny brought Tim to the back room after the store closed so he could see it. Tim asked, "What is that?" and I said, "That's you Chili Nose!" Tim's countenance fell and I almost felt sorry for him. Johnny high-fived me and said, "What's up Chili?" I told him we were tired of working hard only to receive criticism from him. Tim went on to say he was sorry for being so hard on us and offered us a beer. It worked… he was now one of us.

From that point forward, Johnny lost respect for Chili and would hit him on the butt with a rubber band that had been stretched to the point of breaking. Johnny did this while Tim was assisting customers from behind the raised service desk. Johnny liked to see Tim shake in his powder blue polyester pants when the rubber band struck. Since the rubber band flew at Tim from the backside of the service desk, customers did not see it. Tim would say, "Cut that out!" and Johnny would respond, "shut up, Chili!" The inmates were once again in charge of the asylum.

The store had a food heating station with infrared heat lamps. There were many occasions when I heated hot links and ate them during my work shift. I actually paid for these and put a receipt on them as they heated up while I worked. Sometimes customers would want to buy my ready-to-eat meal. When my friends would come to visit me at the store, we would go into the back room and devour some "chomp." One of the things I loved to eat was avocados with Fritos. I remember my buddy

Jimmy Vaughn eating with me several times. There was also one of my friends from Phoenix College named Jenny that also ate in the back room. She was tomboyish but gorgeous and lots of fun to hang out with. She came into the store one day with her eyes crossed and pretended like that was her normal look. I was busy that day and she followed me around with her eyes crossed. It annoyed me at the time but looking back, it is pretty funny. I always wanted to be more than friends with her, but our relationship did not go past our fun times.

One of my favorite memories was the day JD Hill came to visit me at the store. JD Hill was a superstar playing as a wide receiver at Arizona State University. He was drafted in the first round into the NFL and later became a Pro Bowler. I was an avid ASU fan at the time of his visit. While attending Phoenix College, I met an avid Jesus follower who informed me she was my cousin (more on this later). My cousin Carol was engaged to another ASU football player named Calvin who just happened to be best friends with JD Hill. His visit to see me at Carlito's was arranged by Carol through her fiancé Calvin. That day, JD drove up in a custom black Mark IV that had super-dark tinted windows and some custom rims. He was styling and dressed like he was Superfly. He walked into the store like he owned it and much to my surprise started asking the cashiers, "Where's Ruben?" I recognized him immediately and was speechless as I approached him. He said, "Are you Ruben?" and all I could do was nod yes. He shook my hand and went on to say that he heard I was an ASU fan. He gave me one of his ASU football jerseys and I looked at him in disbelief. He laughed and pointed at my shoe and said I had something stuck on it. When I looked down and looked up again, he was laughing and exiting the front door. He pointed at me and said, "Gotcha!" and he jumped into his expensive automobile. That was my best day at Carlito's, and everyone at the store was impressed that the one and only JD Hill would stop by to see me and give me a jersey. At this point I had some serious "barrio cred" (barrio credibility). Thank you again Carol!

Barrio lesson # 19 Drinking is addictive

CHAPTER 20

High School in the Hood

Going from the sheltered environment of Dominguez Seminary to Carl Hayden High School was a total shock to me socially and emotionally. My friend Joe also quit the seminary but went on to St. Mary's High School. Joe had a sister named Christine that attended Carl Hayden. I had seen Christine and her sister Ofelia on several occasions at the CYO functions at church. When they mentioned how cute I was, I said I'm glad you have 20/20 vision. They also told me I was conceited and why do they bother even wasting their time talking to me.

Christine was a senior and captain of the cheerleaders; she was full of spunk and more than boisterous. She took me under her wing and told me she was going to make me the most popular boy in high school. She asked me to share her locker and wrote my name all over her notebooks. She was about 5' 10" tall, and she liked that I was taller than her. She let me know not to get excited as she was pretending to be my girlfriend to make the guy she liked jealous. This tactic must have worked for her because last I heard she is still married to this guy.

At first, I did not know she was a cheerleader and my handful of friends were surprised to find out we were "a couple." She would have me walk her to class and meet by her locker after every class. She introduced me as her boyfriend to all the cheerleaders and pom pom girls. At the football games, I would have to go and pay her a visit at the fence that separated the stands from the football field. It was funny because I would go up to the fence, and we would talk about her brother Joe. She would sometimes whisper in my ear because the guy she liked was watching us. I grew a little bolder and said, "Let's make him really jealous!" and I hugged her tightly. She laughed and said, "Ooh, I like that! But remember, we are just pretending!"

At lunchtime, we would sometimes go over to B&K hamburger stand where lots of kids from our high school hung out. It was fun hanging around the "in" crowd and people that I did not who know would say hello to me. Christine once asked me if I thought she was pretty. I told her yes but added that she was too bony and loud. She laughed it off but as soon as I said it, I could tell I hurt her feelings.

My friend Joe called me shortly after this to find out if I had any interest in his sister, and I told him we were just friends. Just as quickly as our pretend relationship started, it also ended. One day at her locker, she screamed, "Ruben Gonzales! You two-timer! Get out of my locker!" The element of surprise worked out perfectly for her as I tried to figure out what was happening. It was a dramatic breakup and I had to downgrade to the original locker assigned to me. This locker was away from all the popular girls. I later dated one of pom pom girls Christine had introduced me to.

There was a young lady named Annie that would harass me. She hung around with three or four other girls, and when I walked by them, she would say, "Sure wish I had some." They would all laugh as I was shy and freshly out of the priest school. By my senior year, I went up to Annie after getting my nerve up. I said, "Sure wish I had some" but she quickly responded, "Too late, I already got some." She and her friends laughed as I got spammed.

My heart's desire was to play sports at Carl Hayden. The baseball coach begged me to come out for the team after watching me pitch at PE. I also excelled at track and could outrun most of the boys in a footrace. I could not play sports because of my job at Carlito's, and making money was more important to me.

One of the funny things that happened to me happened in the boy's bathroom at school. There was a kid named Chucky who I knew for many years from Jackson Elementary. As I was relieving myself at one of the urinals, Chucky came up to the guy next to me who was also urinating. Chucky turned him quickly so he peed on my leg. I was furious and chased Chucky, but he was too quick. I scrubbed my leg with Ajax before joining my PE class. One of my other friends that we called Bison (RIP) was there, and he told my other friends about the urinal incident and called it "the stain." Chucky would always laugh when he saw me, and I was never able to pay him back. He went on to play basketball with a full scholarship at the University of Oregon.

My friend Bison played football as a walk-on at Arizona State University. He was a Native American who took pleasure in telling me I lived south of the tracks. Bison was one of Coop's friends that always mooched off us since he had no money. He was a big eater and would go with us to Lester's Diner. This was a small diner located in a transformed house trailer with lots of windows. Bison would place and eat a big order and then tell us he had no money. On the last time we went there, Coop and I went to the car when the bill came. We drove around the diner and pointed and laughed at Bison who was stuck with the bill for our food. He pleaded with us and we went back in to pay. Bison was furious as we embarrassed him as we taught him a lesson. Coop was quick to point out that it was my idea as he feared him. When we got into the car, I told him I was tired of him eating whatever he wanted and then we had to pay. He swore to get even with me, and I named this incident "Bison's bill." Bison ended up dying young after contracting hepatitis C. He had a younger brother named Kip, and they lived in the barrio nicknamed minipark.

Late into my junior year in high school, I started dating a girl and we went to the prom. She was the oldest of nine kids that lived near the school in a small two-bedroom house. Whenever I was going to take her out, I would have to go ask her father at the neighborhood bar for permission to take her out. I used to think it was a real crock because if he really cared, he would be home. My mother did not like the idea that my girlfriend was two years older than me. We went around for about a year, and then my brother Papo started dating her sister that I nicknamed Tiger. My prom girlfriend and I broke up almost as soon as Papo and Tiger hooked it up. Tiger was full of fire and got into some serious fights after school.

Prior to meeting my brother, she had a boyfriend named Rick that was a complete hoodlum. This is the same guy I mentioned in an earlier chapter when I scored a knockout. After a couple of years, Tiger and my brother Papo got married and had two wonderful kids Ray III and Nancy. They had a tumultuous marriage that included lots of drinking. At this point, Papo was a crazed Vietnam veteran feeling the effects of post-traumatic stress syndrome, and the VA did not help much back then.

I started drinking on a regular basis on weekends at the age of seventeen with my brothers, uncles, and parents. This was in addition to having beers at the store on a regular basis. It felt like I was missing something, so I drank to fill the void, but it only made it worse. I remember my mother hitting Papo and I with a broom one late night because we were drinking whiskey and making a ruckus late at night in our bedroom. Richard was already married and out of the house at this point. My mother's advice to me again was, "If you are going to drink, at least learn to drink right!" So… guess what? I got better at it. I used Papo's military ID to buy beer at the drive thru liquor store on the corner of 19th Avenue and Van Buren. I would put on his military-issued glasses that blurred my vision and confidently handed over his ID when requested. I remember an old man commenting to his wife about how kids were looking younger and younger as he handed me my six pack of Coors beer. I proudly commented to him, "I've already been to Vietnam and back."

I almost got arrested for underage drinking along with my sister and several other wedding party members. After a rehearsal for Papo's and Tiger's wedding, I took a group to Encanto Park so we could drink. A lone park security guard came up on us and said we were all under arrest. He tried to call the police but was having trouble with his radio. There were ten of us and one of him. I quickly figured out he did not have a gun and he looked scared. He told us we all had to stay confined to an area, so I got everyone in a huddle and told them I would distract the guard so everyone could run. The guard was nervous when I approached him and yelled at me to stop. I continued approaching him and yelling, "What!" with my arms extended out. He told me he was going to handcuff me. I got close enough to him so he could almost touch me, and I told everybody to run. I bumped the guard hard with my shoulder and took off running at half speed so he would think he could catch me. As he got close, I accelerated and went into a zigzag pattern…. I was having fun with him. By this time everyone had made a run for it, and I proceeded to get away from the guard easily. After all I was named Ruben the rabbit. It was fortunate for us that we did not get caught because it was about two miles from the house. I was able to return to my car and round everyone up. In the group was my cousin Maggie who was only about fourteen years old at the time.

During that time, the Vietnam War was raging, and Coop's brother got his leg blown off. I knew I did not want to get drafted into the Army and go into the front lines of this unpopular war. I remember going to antiwar protests at the State Capitol where the Brown Berets would show up and we would chant, "Chicano! Power!" and "Hell no, we won't go!" Robert Kennedy and Martin Luther King got assassinated around this time, and there were lots of civil rights issues.

By this time, I had my 1962 Chevy, and I was so proud of my red and white beauty. It once cost me an exorbitant amount of $6 to fill the gas tank. One of my best days back then was when I went to the gas station on the SE corner of 19th Avenue and Van Buren to a malfunctioning gas pump. The gas came out at normal speed while the amount indicator barely turned. I filled up my car for 37 cents. I quickly headed home and filled up my parent's 1970 Le Mans for less than half a dollar. I tried to fill up my dad's truck, but when I went back for the third time, there was an out of order sign on this gas pump. The gas stations used to give loyalty incentives to their customers. My parents had a nice collection of tall frosted glasses with pictures of some of the local cactus. My favorite was the ocotillo cactus, but the giant saguaro and organ pipe were not far behind.

The only time I ever took my three sisters to the drive-in was on December 31, 1969. It was a nice way to put away the 1960s, and that night was really memorable for all of us and then some. We went to see the *Night of the Living Dead*. It scared the dickens out of me, and I was seventeen years old at the time. So, I figure, the movie scared my sisters for life. Lupe was fifteen, Lydia was nine, and baby girl Anita was only six. When we got home, we slept with the lights on and still saw shadows lurking around.

That night I parked my 1962 Chevy in front of the house. Shortly after midnight, I was awakened by my drunk brother Papo and tipsy cousin Joey. They were laughing and yelling, "Happy New Year!" They proceeded to tell me a drunk driver smashed into the back of my car and they thought it was hilarious. I didn't believe it until I saw the red and blue lights from a police car flashing in front of our house. The drunk driver was already handcuffed in the back seat of the police car. To add insult to injury, I watched Joey snap off the antenna from my hard-earned vehicle as they celebrated and continued laughing.

The person that hit my car had insurance and my vehicle was subsequently repaired. The insurance would not cover the broken antenna, and I had a difficult time finding a replacement at the junkyard and installing it properly. My music in the car and the song in my heart were altered that early morning on January 1, 1970. The year certainly started with a bang.

My graduation ceremony from Carl Hayden was long and somewhat boring. At the end of the ceremony, we did the traditional graduation cap toss into the air. Prior to throwing mine into the air, I removed my tassel and placed it securely in my pocket. When I picked a hat, it had a tassel attached to it, so I ended up with two tassels from the CHHS class of 1970. I apologize to my classmate that ended up with my tassel-less hat. Hope you were able to obtain another one without having to graduate again. After graduating from high school in 1970, I enrolled into Phoenix College and attended for one year. My parents discouraged me from going to college and thought it was a waste of my time. It was an unsure time in my life because my parents were pushing me to get a real job. I wanted to become a special education (PE) teacher. There was also the uncertainty of the annual draft lottery that was like an ominous cloud following every step that I took.

You may have noticed there is no scripture in this chapter as I had fallen into a downward spiral. My life had turned complicated and I was confused by everything. I wanted to succeed by going to school but had no clue how to begin my career path. Maybe I could join the Navy? Join the circus? No, joining the circus was not an option because I already worked there at Carlito's Market.

I can't leave this chapter without sharing my favorite verse in the Bible. Jesus said, "I am vine and you are the branches. If a man abides in me and I in him, he will bear much fruit. Apart from me, you can do nothing" (John 15:5).

Barrio lesson #20 Drinking is a way of life

CHAPTER 21

BALL OF CONFUSION

In September of 1970, I enrolled at Phoenix College. Only a couple of my friends from Carl Hayden enrolled at PC. One of them was Mary Bug and her shadow Katie. I knew Mary from Our Lady of Fatima and we made our first communion together. Mary used to bug me for rides to Phoenix College and we had one class together. I made her cry once because I copied her homework and turned mine in but not hers. She had a "crutch" on one of my buddies named Raul. I say crutch because that was my corny joke I used by telling my friends, "See that guy over there, he has a crutch on you." When they looked up to see who it was, the person was on crutches. Crutch is how a vato with a strong Spanish accent would say crush while he ate his shicken. Anyway, Mary Bug wanted to meet Raul.

I told her to meet me at the top of the stairs at a pre-arranged time near one of the classes that Raul and I attended. When I introduced them, somehow Mary lost her balance and did an emergency tap dance down the stairs. She was able to stay on her feet but crashed into the wall at the bottom of the stairs. Once I knew she was okay, I laughed and called out to her, "Other than that, Mrs. Lincoln, how did you like the play?" It was hysterical, and for a couple of days, I did not have to give Mary Bug a ride home as she became a missing person.

I met some good friends at PC and enjoyed the competitive football games during the PE class. One of my best friends was Bill who had a girlfriend named Rosa. They were getting serious about each other until Bill had to go to the Big House. Bill called me once late on a Saturday night and told me to come help him get out of a mess. He was in the Campito barrio and had run over a dog and crashed into a telephone pole. He said to hurry as the dog owners were plenty upset with him. I showed up with my Louisville Slugger and helped him escape this rough neighborhood. He was grateful as he was certain a couple of the thugs were about to ruin his evening. We stopped by Jack in the Crack, and I lectured him on the dangers of drinking and driving; it was like the jalapeno calling the frog green. Bill settled down after he had to pay for a telephone pole. Bill and Rosa soon got engaged, but that no good alcohol took over. He was involved in a fatal automobile accident and convicted of manslaughter while intoxicated. It is my understanding he spent seven years incarcerated and I never saw him again.

I saw his younger sister many times when I picked her up from high school while I was on leave from the Navy. She offered me some "pudding" that I could not eat at a secluded spot near the Verde River. I couldn't believe what I saw when I got back from "draining the weasel" (urinating) to our picnic spot. She was spread out on the blanket wearing nothing but a smile. Believe me, my body was willing, but my spirit and better judgment prevailed as I had no raincoat. It was not the right time for this as I was on leave from the Navy and she was ditching that day from high school. We were both lonely, but the chemistry between us was not quite there. She was a firecracker who was looking for a way to leave her parent's house and authority.

During that year at Phoenix College, I had no sense of vision or encouragement from my parents to go to school. I met my cousin Carol and she told me her mother and my father were first cousins. My Tia Chayo (my great aunt) is my paternal grandmother's sister and Carol's grandmother. Carol was a Jesus freak who most of us avoided. She came up to me and one day said, "Hey, I think you are my cousin." She used to try to tell me about Jesus back then, but I was not old enough yet. My time would come, I just didn't know when, but God always knew the day and the place even if it was almost thirty years later.

I hung around with Carol and her friend Susan on a regular basis. We went everywhere in Susan's Volkswagen, and I installed an eight-track tape player into it. We sang the heck out of Carole King's *Tapestry* album along with anything by Sly and the Family Stone. Cheech and Chong were in their heyday and we were young and enjoying life. We would make an impromptu drive to the river with a group of friends and enjoyed some Strawberry Hill from our leather wine bags.

Around this time, I was introduced to another vice to help me cram for finals. It was first a product called No Doz but it upset my stomach. My drinking was getting the better of me, and it was hard for me to stay awake. One of my lowbrow friends showed me how he mixed alcohol with some "white crosses" (amphetamines). Presto! And now in front of you, there is a wide awake drunk. If any of you reading this are doing this, *you must stop!* It is like playing Russian roulette with all the chambers full.

I had an experience where during one of these drinking sessions, my brain seemed to short-circuit. I closed my eyes and saw static, like when the television loses signal. It scared me, and for a moment, I wasn't sure if my brain would reconnect. I regretted doing this as I betrayed myself and boasted how alcohol did not affect me. I almost did not pass my first physical examination for the Navy as my blood pressure was too high. The darkness I was in at this point in my life was so dark I could almost feel it. "Then the Lord said to Moses, 'Stretch out your hand toward the sky so that darkness spreads over Egypt – darkness that can be felt.'"

Meanwhile back at the house, one of the young thugs from my hood sold me some tools at a reasonable price for working on my car. He told me his father had bought a new set of tools and sold me his father's old set. Within a week, the police were knocking on my parent's door. This crazy kid had stolen the tools from someone's garage and sold them to me. My set of tools was confiscated, and I was out fifteen dollars. The young thief told me he would pay me back. That was the last time I saw him as he avoided me like I had toxic radiation looking for a place to land.

Carol, my newfound cousin, used to tease me because I was dating the pom pom girl from Carl Hayden. The pom pom girl was a tall and attractive; she had big brown eyes like Natalie Wood. We had met up by chance at the Riverside ballroom and slow-danced to "Color My World" sung by Ray Camacho. My sister Lupe did not like her and told me she was just using me. I remember telling Lupe we were just using each other. One day, the pom pom girl brought her mother to Carlito's to meet me. She looked stunning as she walked toward me near the dairy aisle in her tailored white dress. We went on several dates and had lots of fun together. We both loved going to Big Surf at night. Big Surf was a water park that attracted lots of people trying to escape the desert heat. The summer nights were hot, but the water was sensational with endless waves. She could not swim, so I had to help her keep her head above water as the waves created by the man-made ocean rise and fall. We held on to each other in the water that was over our shoulders. She was a stunning hot tamale and a credit to her gender.

On one of our dates, we went to a party that we left early so we could talk. I knew of a secluded spot in Encanto Park. Lots can happen when the windows get fogged up and you're the only two people around for miles. Her mother scolded me the next day for putting a slight mark on her daughter's neck. After the car window fogging session at Encanto Park, my feelings for her skyrocketed. I even agreed to paint the trim on their house during the summertime in Phoenix. As I worked, my girl would appear like a genie throughout the day to offer some water or lemonade. I would run from my house on Sherman to their house as I was getting ready for Navy boot camp.

Her mother tried to pay me for painting the house, but I would not accept it. Her grandfather owned a shoe store and gave me a pair of Ked's sneakers that I wore when I left for the Navy. My girl once came with me to my house to meet my mom and dad. We stopped under the mistletoe that was there from Christmas past. My mother later commented that I was getting too serious, too fast. I remember being embarrassed because the ceiling on the front porch was leaking and the plaster was falling off.

Our romance came to a sudden stop after an incident that caused me a great deal of embarrassment. It came at Raymond's wedding shower that took place at American Legion Post 41. Margaret's ex-boyfriend showed up, and my father tripped him as he walked by. An off-duty police officer that had been hired apprehended my father and took him outside. My father was uncooperative, so the officer took him down on the street to place handcuffs on him. I became furious and rushed over and pushed the police officer and screamed, "His back is hurt, quit being so rough!" My brother Richard got into a wrestling match with an officer who had arrived on a motorcycle. There were lots of chaos and commotion as several other officers arrived and began spraying Mace. It was something I regret being in the middle of and will not elaborate on my part in this free for all.

Things changed very quickly from a festive party to a mini riot. When I got some Mace in my face, I backed off, and from out of nowhere, there was my pom pom girl and her mom telling me to stay back. They wiped the Mace from my face, and I told her mom they were hurting my father's back. Her mom calmed me down and told me there is nothing I can do. She said, "If you get in there again, you will be arrested, and you can forget the Navy!" When I heard those words, it made me stop.

My father and brother Richard were placed into the paddy wagon and taken away. I have a vivid memory of my Nana Pipi pounding on the side of the paddy wagon and calling the police officers pigs. We were fortunate not to have more family members arrested, especially me. After that incident, my girl was not permitted to go out with me again.

The song that epitomized what was going on in my world at that point was sung by The Temptations. It was called "Ball of Confusion." Everything was spinning so fast and going nowhere.

Bail was posted so my dad and brother could be released from jail. We had an influential neighbor that was good friends with a judge. Prior to going into the courtroom, this neighbor was able to work some magic, and the case was dismissed with all charges dropped. After the Judge tapped his gavel, my mother described how "our" attorney calmly read his newspaper while the opposing attorney stormed out of the courtroom.

I was having lots of trouble with my car battery and the workers at

Checker Auto Parts got tired of me returning new drained out batteries that were still under warranty. So, my friend Coop and I decided to get a permanent fix for this. We decided to go get a good battery from a newer car at a five-finger discount from one of the better neighborhoods. We borrowed his father's bolt cutters and must of really looked out of place carrying a pair of bolt cutters at twilight.

When we found a new Cadillac under a carport and were just about to open the hood, a man came out of his house holding a shotgun. He yelled, "What the hell are you doing?" We dropped the bolt cutters and ran into his backyard. We started jumping over fences as quickly as we could. It is sheer terror when you are running blindly and about to hear a shotgun blast. All that was missing was a helicopter overhead playing, "Bad boys! Bad boys! What you gonna do… when they come after you?" As we crossed our third yard, there was a trail of barking dogs and backlights being turned on. We were still running at full speed when I barely ducked under a clothesline. Coop got snagged around his neck, and it yanked him to the ground. I heard him go, "Awwwkkk!" I thought about leaving him but went back to help him to his feet. He was having trouble breathing, but we knew we had to keep going. Once we jumped over the fence at the end of the block, we walked normally as if we were taking a leisurely walk through NYC Central Park. It was another stupid gamble on our walk of shame.

Just before leaving for the Navy, I had partied with my Brown Bro one evening. On our way home, we hit a street sign and had to speed off. It was not a serious accident, but I could not afford a DUI on my record. As we drove fast through our hood, I ran over a large dog and felt badly as I saw the dog in my rearview mirror lift his head and then lay down.

At this point in my life, the Navy could not come soon enough for me. I needed to get out of the barrio as fast as I could before I ended up behind bars.

Barrio lesson # 21 If your life is out of control, change your environment

CHAPTER 22

NAVY TO THE RESCUE

During that year at Phoenix College, I was floundering. My grades were not the best, and I spent most of my time in the student union building. This is where the slackers hung out instead of going to class. My passion has always been playing sports, so I really enjoyed engaging in a pickup game of football and basketball whenever possible. I was still working at Carlito's in the evenings, and they were kind enough to match my work and college schedule.

Around this time, we had a neighbor named Tommy who lived next door. Tommy wore thirty-four-inch jeans under his beach ball-sized stomach. When he laughed, "Ho! Ho! Ho!", he sounded just like the Mexican Santa Claus. He had a dog named Coyote pronounced as koy-yoh-teh. That's how you say this mangy dog's name in Spanish. Coyote was a yappy mutt that was a mixture of a Chihuahua and dachshund; I used to call it a chihweenie dog. I never liked Coyote because he was a barking alarm clock that announced to the world what time I got home after going out.

He was a cowardly dog that acted like Rin Tin Tin when Tommy was close by. Anyway, Tommy would always brag about how obedient and well-trained Coyote was. He could make the dog stand on his back legs at his command. Tommy would yell "parate Coyote" (stand up Coyote) and the dog would stand like a statue until Tommy gave him the command to go down to all fours. Tommy would tell me his dog would not move no matter what until he gave the release command.

One time when Tommy was drinking, I told him he did not have complete control over Coyote as I saw him roaming the neighborhood earlier that day. He quickly called Coyote and scolded him for leaving the yard. He demonstrated his control over the mutt by making the dog stand while he backed his car just a few inches from running over him. It was hilarious to see Coyote shaking and even peeing in fear, but he would not move. You could almost see beads of dog sweat as Tommy barked out, "Aye quedate Coyote y no te muevas!" (You stay there Coyote and don't you move). No matter how close the tires got to Coyote, he stayed standing on his back legs. It was unbelievable and Tommy proved his control over Coyote that day. Life is tough when you're a barrio dog.

My friend Coop had a set of friends that lived in the minipark barrio. They used to like to smoke pot, and I did not care much to hang out with them. There was a couple of times that I stopped by with Jimmy and the guys were all jacked up. I asked them if they were hungry, and they said they had some serious "munchies." They were always broke, and they salivated when I offered to go to Jack in the Box for them. They placed their orders that included several jack tacos. I would say I'll be back but never returned. Their memory was not the best, and they lost track of when I would return. I never did like being around a group of guys smoking pot, so I messed with them. I stuck to drinking beer and Strawberry Hill.

During this time, I was always trying to figure out ways to make extra cash without having sticky fingers at the cash register or selling drugs. There were a couple of young hoodlums from the projects that I would give rides to for the price of bus fare. They were both about fifteen years old. On one of these rides, they asked me if I could drop them off and pick them up after an hour at a local nightclub parking lot on the upcoming Saturday night. They offered me twenty dollars to do it. They said, "To make it easier for you, we will show you where to meet us afterward." It sounded like an easy way to make twenty dollars and my Saturday was open. They sweetened the pot by offering me an eight-track player for my vehicle and would even install it. I dropped them off and went for a ride keeping an eye on the time. They told me it was really important for me to be there exactly an hour later to pick them up. When I approached our designated meeting location, I saw the two young hoodlums running for their lives as three men chased them. I saw them get taken down to the ground as I left the scene like I was a car just passing by.

I figured it out—these two young jokers were breaking into cars and stealing eight track players. I was naïve enough to take them there and be their getaway car. I felt badly leaving, but I did not want to go to jail as I was over eighteen while both were still minors. I feared the police showing up at my house that night. It almost seemed liked there was an ominous cloud floating in my dark bedroom that night. It was awful to have fear and anxiety working together in as my mind to convince me the guys would tell the police I took them there. Being a person with an unsure sense of what will happen next locks you in a prison of paranoia.

I was on the verge of getting into serious trouble as my drinking was out of control. My former best friend Jimmy Vaughn was already in prison for armed robbery. Coop and I had almost gotten caught attempting to steal a car battery. Brown Bro and I had hit a street sign and killed a dog after a night of drinking. I had been involved with an altercation with the police. I had purchased stolen property. What else could happen? I guess you could say I was no longer the good kid fresh out of the seminary. I was living the vida loca (crazy life). I'm glad God loves us so much—He will never give up on us even if we are about to give up on ourselves.

There was a lottery for the draft and my number was somewhere in the teens out of 365. So, I decided to join the Navy rather than being drafted by the Army. I enlisted in the Navy in the spring of 1971 with my first active duty date scheduled for September 21, 1971, and reporting to San Diego. I was guaranteed an "A" school after boot camp. "A" school means they will train you in an area that best fits the results of your Navy aptitude testing. I also had to commit to a six-year enlistment term that included two years of active reserve duty.

I stopped working at the beginning of September so I could enjoy the last few days prior to leaving my childhood home and barrio. It was boring to stay at home, so I did responsible things like giving my sisters and their two friends Sandy and Shelly a ride to school at St. Matthew's and picking them up in the afternoon. One time when the girls were getting into the car, I reached to pull the seat forward as my sister Anita was getting in. She said, "Ow, you hit my nose!" I quickly responded, "That was your nose, I thought it was a pickle!" She buried her head in her pleated skirt (Catholic school uniform) and cried all the way to school. I felt kind of bad about it, but it was humorous at the time. I publicly apologize to Anita now after nearly forty-eight years for saying that.

In the afternoon, after picking them up from school, I deviated from the direct route home. I took my sisters and their friends through the enormous Greenwood Cemetery near the freeway on Van Buren. I would pretend to be lost but I knew my way around pretty well from my paper punk days. The girls did not know for sure if I knew how to get out of the cemetery. I was doing them a favor because I was developing their fortitude and helping their sense of direction while terrorizing them. I somehow knew life would never be the same again after I left for the Navy. It was my way to leave them with a special memory of me.

Going into the Navy was exactly what I needed to take a break from the things I was doing and to grow up. It was the second chance at life that God provided for me since I was floundering on my own. "For I know the plans I have for you, declares the Lord, plans for welfare and not evil, to give you a future and a hope" (Jeremiah 29:11).

On September 21, 1971, I left Phoenix Sky Harbor International Airport en route to San Diego. There were several of my Phoenix College friends along with my parents who went to see me off at the airport. I wore a red, white, and blue patriotic shirt along with a big white star in the center of my chest. My pants were white with blue and red stripes. Even my tennis shoes were red, white, and blue. It felt good to be of Mexican descent but displaying my colors like a proud American ready to serve his country. Once I was on the plane, I felt very alone and knew my life was about to drastically change…. *My barrio walk was now officially complete.*

My military-issued orders had me reporting to the Marine on Duty at the San Diego International Airport no later than 1600 or 4 pm. I arrived at the San Diego airport around 1 pm. I quickly observed some other new Navy recruits being tormented by abusive Marines. They called them worms and let the recruits know they owned them. The new recruits were made to stand with their faces about an inch away from the wall. The young Geester (me) knew he wanted to delay the Marine abuse as long as possible. I pretended to be just another traveler and explored the San Diego airport for almost three extra hours of freedom. The Marines kept looking at me as I strolled by in my patriotic clothes. I was strutting like a rooster as I was not "officially" late until 4 pm. When I turned in my enlistment orders to the Marines at 3:55 pm, they were pissed that I was able to delay my civilian status for more than two extra hours. The two Marines berated me for a solid five minutes beginning at 3:55 pm as I chuckled inside. Right at 4 pm, they herded about a dozen of us toward our next stop at "worm island."

I remember looking back sadly at the gates of the Naval Training Station knowing my life had just completely changed. It was a sad first night in the barracks, and I could hear a few guys crying. The night did not last very long. We were rudely awakened by a trash can being thrown into the barracks at 4:30 am. The Marine rooster yelled, "Get up you worthless worms!" We had to be shaved, bed made, and dressed for breakfast within minutes. We were Company 319 and our platoon leader was a Filipino drill instructor with the last name of Bautista. He was a serious man and his mantra was "Make it so!" He could have used the phrase "Just do it," but it already belonged to Nike.

The next and final chapter is a story in itself about my father during his last days on earth. It is one I hope you will read in entirety as things in this chapter happened in 2002. This chapter is very personal to me, and I wrote it while crying and praying for the right words to describe properly and exactly how it happened. It demonstrates what can happen to any of us when we make the right decision. God knows us better than anyone and loves us more than anyone ever could.

Ruben M. Gonzales, Viet Nam Veteran
Served as Radioman on the USS Gray DE-1054

Barrio lesson # 22 When you have an appointment to pick up hoodlums, make sure you know they were not committing a crime just before you pick them up.

CHAPTER 23

DAD: JUMP!

My father was dying but did not know it. His health and strength were dwindling away slowly out of his body like a clogged-up drain. About two months before his passing away, I took a week off from work as Postmaster in McAllen, TX. We went to see his cardiologist, and the doctor told him, "There is nothing I can do for you but at least you won't have to make another appointment with me." It was an awful feeling driving him home and not knowing what to say. My father went home in good spirits and announced to my mother, "See I told you there was nothing wrong with me. The doctor told me I did not need to make another appointment."

Right then I realized my father had no clue that his life was almost over. I chuckle when I think about his favorite questions to me over the last few years of his life. He would ask me, "Do you think I'm gonna make it, man?" He worked so hard all his life in the fields, served in the Army during World War II, spent thirty years or more working at the City of Phoenix, and then worked another ten years at the USPS as the best custodian in postal history. It seemed like throughout his life, the only time he did not work was when he was sleeping. He collected scrap iron, cut yards and performed handy man jobs as long as I can remember.

A couple of days after seeing the doctor, my mother and sister had some errands to run, so it was my turn to stay with him. Both my mom and my sister thought I was weird as I had recently become a born-again Christian. They were totally against the fact that I did not attend Catholic church anymore. We had several heated discussions over praying to statues and saying rosaries. I had to use the phrase, "We need to agree to disagree" to end these discussions. My father was in bed because he was too tired to get up. When I went into his room, he was having a difficult time trying to make sense on his inability to get out of bed. He told me, "If only I could eat a little bit, I know I would feel better." He looked through his bedroom window at his citrus trees and said, "Look at my lemon trees; I need to get out there and pull the grass that is growing around them." At that moment, two birds hopped joyfully onto the windowsill. I told him, "Dad, look at those two birds, they don't worry about anything." He growled at me and snapped, "What are you talking about man?" I remained calmed and said, "Let me show you."

I opened my bible to Luke 12:24–26 and read, "Consider the ravens: they do not sow or reap, they have no storeroom or barn; yet God feeds them. And how much more valuable you are than those birds! Who of you by worrying can add a single hour to your life? Since you cannot do this very little thing, why do you worry about the rest?" He looked at me and said, "I didn't know that was in there."

I asked him if he wanted me to show him more and he nodded yes, so I quickly flipped the pages of my bible to John 14:1–6. I explained to him Jesus was saying goodbye to His disciples as He knew he was about to be crucified. "Jesus said, 'Do not let your hearts be troubled. You believe in God; believe also in me. My Father's house has many rooms; if that were not so, would I have told you that I am going there to prepare a place for you? And if I go and prepare a place for you, I will come back and take you to be with me that you also may be where I am. You know the way to the place where I am going.' Thomas said to him, 'Lord, we don't know where you are going, so how can we know the way?' Jesus answered, 'I am the way the truth and the life. No one comes to the Father except through me.'"

My father looked surprised and said, "I didn't know that was in there." I asked him if he wanted me to show him more, and he said yes as he sat up a little higher like a child being read a bedtime story. The good book does say that in order to get to heaven, we must be like little children. (while writing this part of the story, I became very emotional and had to pray to Jesus to help me finish writing it) My fingers sped to the Book of Romans 10: 9–10, 13. I read to him: "If you declare with your mouth, 'Jesus is Lord,' and believe in your heart that God raised him from the dead, you will be saved. For it is with your heart that you believe and are justified, and it is with your mouth that you profess your faith and are saved…. for, 'Everyone who calls on the name of the Lord will be saved.'" At this point, my father's eyes were bright and focused. I asked him, "You believe Jesus is Lord, right? And you believe that God raised him from the dead, right?" He replied yes to both questions, so I asked him if he wanted to hear more and said, "Sure!"

We moved to the last chapter Revelation 3: 20 and I read: "Here I am! I stand at the door and knock. If anyone hears my voice and opens the door, I will come in and eat with that person, and they with me." I paused and told my father Jesus was knocking on the door of his heart. I asked him if he wanted to invite Jesus into his heart as his Lord and Savior, and he said yes. So, we bowed our heads and he repeated a simple prayer asking for forgiveness, acknowledging Jesus as Lord, and thanking God for raising Jesus and us from the dead.

When I looked at my father, he had a goofy smile on his face. For the first time I could ever remember, he even looked kind of nerdy. He asked me, "Do you think I'll make it, man?" I smiled and replied, "You already have." We hugged each other, and he told me I was a good son; I felt like my heart was about to explode because it was so full of joy. He slept peacefully that afternoon, and my mother asked me if I had given him something to help him sleep. I told her I had not, but little did she know that he had received a healthy dose of the gos-pill.

During the next two months at my job back in McAllen, my siblings were upset with me because I did not take off from work to be with them as dad continued to weaken. On March 14, 2002, around noon, my sister Anita called me and said, "You need to come home now! Hospice said dad only has twenty-four to forty-eight hours to live." So, we packed up the Riviera and left for the twenty-hour drive from McAllen, Texas, to Phoenix at 1 pm. The drive was difficult, but Anthony helped me when I needed it most at about 2 am. Irma struggled to keep us both awake as she would sometimes fall asleep in the middle of her singing. The stress from the emotions and the long drive seemed insurmountable…so we praised! We reached Tucson around 8 am; I thought daylight would make it better, but it only got worse. The drive was physically and emotionally draining to the three of us.

We arrived at my parent's house shortly after 9 am. When we walked undetected through the open garage, there was an awkward silence in the room like they had been talking about me. My father was in a coma-like sleep, but he smiled when he heard my voice and that made me feel good. That day, we all stayed by his bedside and talked with him. I knew he could still hear me, so I was able to express my love for him. I even forgave him for the time he had me pull the spark plug wire off the faulty lawn mower while it was still running. I did not know he used a small stick to dislodge the spark plug wire. That lesson in the school of hard knocks gave me the shock of my life and hurt my finger and feelings as a young boy.

Irma and I sang songs to him throughout the day. During the Christmas holidays, he loved to hear us sing "Silent Night." At the end of the song, he clapped and then asked us to sing it in Spanish and we would. Later in the day, my sister asked us and other visitors to leave him alone as he needed to rest. My mind screamed, "Rest from what?", but my self-control kept my mouth shut… thank God.

That night at about 9:15 pm, my sister Anita, who had been his primary caretaker, announced to my father that she was leaving. She told him she would be back to see him in the morning. At that moment, my father began to struggle for breath. We (mom, Anita, Ernie, and I) rushed to his bedside. My sister said, "It's okay daddy, the angels are all around you." She even rang the small bells of the angel wind chimes that were dangling above his bed. Then a miracle happened. I leaned in close to my father and said, "Dad, jump into Jesus' arms!" My father, who had been out all day in a coma-like state, sat up and reached out.... He took three last gasps and he was gone. It was the most beautiful, surreal moment of my life. There was so much peace and tranquility in the room that is beyond my understanding. I felt like liquid love, peace and joy had been poured over me. It was the closest I had ever been to the Prince of Peace when my father reached out to Him.

Remarkable. His salvation did not come from praying to the saints or rubbing beads. He did not say a novena to St. Anthony Claret. He did not have to confess his sins to a priest or say a prayer five times per day. Like Jesus said, "No one comes to the Father except through me." I close this book with boldness by re-emphasizing the words found in 1 Timothy 2:5: "For there is one God and one mediator between God and mankind, the man Christ Jesus."

Life lesson # 1 Accept Jesus as Lord and Savior early in your life.

Thank you for walking with me through my barrio.

Stay with me as we continue taking steps into Wisdom...

CPSIA information can be obtained
at www.ICGtesting.com
Printed in the USA
LVHW081430141119
637356LV00007B/21/P